Horse Tales
& Hunt Talk

The Life and Times of 31 Equestrians

In Ireland, America, France and Australia

By Noel Mullins

Published in Ireland by
NDM Publications
Old Barrack House
Malheney
Skerries
County Dublin
Ireland

Distributed by NDM Publications

© Noel Mullins 2006

E-mail: noelmullins@hotmail.com

The moral right of the author has been asserted.

A catalogue record of this book is available from the British Library.

ISBN 0-9554364-0-0
978-0-9554364-0-6

Design and Typeset Artwerk Limited

Printed By ColourBooks Limited

Dedication

This Book is dedicated to my family, my wife Emer, daughter
Sheila, and my son Philip, and especially to my mother Mary
Josephine Mullins, who was an enthusiastic follower of the
Galway Blazers. She was a very positive influence on my life
with horses and hounds.

Acknowledgments

I am grateful to the following people who assisted me with information and their time in writing this book, most especially the subjects and their connections. I would also thank them for their permission to use photographs, and images of paintings.

Alison and June Baker, Bill Bourns, Toni de la Bouillerie, Tommy Brennan, George Briscoe, Dick Cahill, George Chapman, Pam Chapman, Jan Cruickshank, Joe Curtis, Chantal Deon, Michael Dempsey, Ann Derwin, Jim Derwin, Ivan Dowling, Eamonn Dunphy, Siobhan English, Kevin Gates of the Australian Racing Museum, Nancy Penn Smith Hannum, Lady Anne Hemphill, Lord Peter Patrick Hemphill, Oonagh Mary Hyland, Iris Kellett, Catherine Camoran-Kennedy, Jack Lambert, Willie Leahy, Dorethy Leahy, Hugh Leonard, Morgan Llywelyn, Margaret Lynch, Paddy Lynch, John Masterton, Jim Meads (Photographer), John Minoprio (Photographer), Cyril Smith, John Stafford, Elsie Morgan, Tom Morgan, Emer Mullins, Philip Mullins, Sheila Mullins, Des McCheane, Dave McConchie, Gerry McGarry, Margie McLoone, Shirley Ringling North, Pat O'Brien, Aidan O'Connell, James O'Connor, Charlie O'Neill, John Pickering, Catherine Power, Paul Ronan, Anne Ryan, Chris Ryan, Thady Ryan, Finbar Ryan, Lorraine Scully, Maxie Scully, Rosemary Skrine, Dr John Waldron, Florrie Webb, Fiona Wentges, Captain John Wentges, Michael Wentges, Pakie Whelan, Grania Willis.

Contents

Book Illustrations

Illustrations and Photos courtesy of

Book Cover	Author
Author Noel Mullins	Joe Curtis
Lady Molly Cusack-Smith	Lady Anne Hemphill
Grania Willis	Author
Elsie Morgan	Jim Meads The Sportsman's Photographer
Tommy Brennan	The Irish Field
Florrie Webb	Author
John Huston	Lady Anne Hemphill
Nancy Penn Smith Hannum	Nancy Penn Smith Hannum
Toni de la Bouillerie	Author
Alison Baker	Alison Baker
Francie Derwin	Ann Derwin
Willie Leahy	Author
Thady Ryan	Catherine Power
Michael Dempsey	Author
George Briscoe	Author
Hugh Leonard	Hugh Leonard
Pat O'Brien	Author
Rosemary Skrine	Author
Eamonn Dunphy	Author
John Pickering	John Pickering
Maxie Scully	Gerry McGarry
Morgan Llywelyn	Morgan Llywelyn
Jack Lambert	Author
Charlie O'Neill	Author
Captain John Wentges	Captain John Wentges
Bill Bourns	Author
Chantal Deon	Author
Lady Anne Hemphill	Oonagh Mary Hyland
Iris Kellett	Irish Independent Newspapers
Aidan O'Connell	Author
Stanislaus Lynch	Margaret Lynch
George Watson	Jan Cruickshank
Additional Feature Photography	Author

Photographic Year

All photos except the following	Author
Print of George Watson	Painted by Frederick Woodhouse Senior 1820 -1909. Courtesy of Mr. John Masterton and Mr. Jeff Urie Joint Masters of The Melbourne Hunt.
Aidan O'Connell and Suave	John Minoprio Photography
Author and Peter O'Toole	Sheila Mullins
Author and Kevin McGuinness	Sheila Mullins

Preface

If anybody is of the opinion that there are no more characters in the horse world then just read Noel Mullins' new book 'Horse Tales & Hunt Talk, and it will soon dispel that view. Sadly a few of the heroes of his book have passed away in the last few years, but most are hail, hearty and still hunting.

It would be hard to imagine a serious account of legendary Irish hunting characters without including Lady Molly Cusack-Smith or Thady Ryan. Others that are featured like Rosemary Skrine and Michael Dempsey have been honoured by the IMFA, each for their lifelong contribution to hunting. Iris Kellett and Tommy Brennan have been outstanding ambassadors in Showjumping and Eventing, and Lady Anne Hemphill for her contribution to Connemara Pony breeding. In each case Noel provides a welcome and fresh look at their exploits.

Others that have served hunting, eventing and showjumping well are Grania Willis as a full time equestrian journalist in the national press. Her personal achievement of climbing the North Face of Mount Everest in her book *Total High* is a story of enormous significance. Another person of inspiration was Maxie Scully who sadly passed away recently. He achieved remarkable success in creating a new World Bareback Highjumping Record as well as being an outstanding athlete in the Transplant Games track and field events, in the face of serious medical adversity.

The inclusion of several international hunting, dressage and racing figures from Australia, America and other European countries gives 'Horse Tales & Hunt Talk 'a broader perspective and appeal.

I have had the pleasure of meeting many of the characters in Noel's book, and he tells their stories of courage, of talent, and inevitably with humour in abundance. He is one of the few writers with the credentials to have attempted such a book. Years of writing hunt reports and features for *The Irish Field* and other international publications have provided him with the opportunity to meet and get to know many of the personalities he has written about. His years of hunting hounds has given him an insight to fully understand hounds and hunting. His passion for the sport and his talent as a writer have all gelled to create not just a witty and fascinating account of hunting characters, but ultimately to have also written this book 'Horse Tales & Hunt Talk' which is a thoroughly good and entertaining read.

Kate Horgan
Master of the Duhallow Foxhounds and
Chairman of the Irish Masters of Foxhounds Association.

Foreword

Dear Reader

It gives me great pleasure to write this foreword to Horse Tales and Hunt Talk, which draws from a worldwide set of equestrian characters. Considering what some of them got up to, it is somewhat surprising that many of them lived as long as they did. The book features the departed, those about to depart, and those with no intention of departing, and you will discover the lives of those who have really influenced the horse world.

Firstly the author gives due recognition to them for their achievements, and secondly succeeding generations will now know more about them. Thirdly their stories have now been recorded before gross exaggeration sets in.

It is great to see horsemen and women from the United States of America being recognised for their generosity to the equestrian world, especially hunting, as many packs would have folded had it not been for their support.

Most of these people devoted their whole lives to their sport, thereby contributing to the continuity, and the endless enjoyment we all derive from it.

Michael Higgens

Author Note

Michael Higgens was Master and Huntsman to The Tipperary Foxhounds for 19 seasons. He was also master and huntsman of the Island Foxhounds, the East Galway Foxhounds, the Ormond Foxhounds, the Avondhu Foxhounds and the Kilmoganny Hounds.

He also represented Ireland in eventing.

Introduction

It has been an interesting journey writing over a period of three years about the 31 subjects in this book, and no doubt there are many more worthy of inclusion. The equestrian world has many personalities, and because I have been meeting many of them since I was quite young, it was probably inevitable that I would at some time compile a snapshot of some, and their interesting lives.

Although I spent much of my career as head of marketing for the computer services company IBM in Ireland, I have always maintained close contact with the horse world through hunting, showjumping and cross country riding. It is a fascinating world for those interested in people, especially as it contains such a broad spread of personalities.

I have been associated with ponies and horses for over 50 years, following my home pack the Galway Blazers Foxhounds as a child, thanks to the generosity of people like Josie Morgan the local milkman, who was kind enough to allow me to go hunting on his milk dray pony, after I had helped him with his milk-rounds of course! It was great fun working the ponies around the farm to take turf home from the bog, and saving the hay.

Commandant Dinny Lundon from Kilcolgan allowed me to ride his showjumping ponies, and I can recall nights clipping them with the non electric hand clippers in the snug of his country pub in Kilcolgan, County Galway, while the ponies' hair was blown around the bar every time a customer opened the front door! The customers used to keep one hand over their pints of beer, and only lift it when they were taking a mouthfull! But they never complained, and conversations just went on as if everything was normal.

1

Michael Dempsey the master of the Galway Blazers who I feature in this book got me my first saddle when he saw me trying to hunt bareback at a meet at what is now Willie Leahy's Horse Museum at Dartfield. He also let me hunt a beautiful grey cob, which was my first introduction to riding horses. In contrast to clipping ponies in Lundon's Pub, I helped Dempsey to clip horses in film director John Huston's stables when he lived at St. Clerans. We still used the hand clippers, but the hospitality was on a different level. I recall on one occasion a member of Mr. Huston's house staff dressed in a black uniform, with a matching white lace apron and head piece who was kind enough to serve us tea in china cups on a silver tray in the stables!

Willie Leahy who you can also read about, that well known horseman and breeder of Connemara ponies also had an influence on my life with horses, as together with my friend Pat O'Neill we used to hack his hirelings to the meets in the days before the ordinary man owned a horse trailer, and an era when there was little traffic on the roads. I again met many interesting people who came to Galway to hunt on Willie's hirelings. They were fit horses in those days, as we regularly hacked 20 miles to a meet, hunt all day, and hack 20 miles home. We were as tired and hungry as the horses, often getting back to the stables after 9 o'clock at night, as Willie was not known for taking a picnic basket with him!

My mother Mary Josephine Higgins had a photographic memory for people and stories, and hunted with the Galway Blazers in her younger days, as did her brother Brendan. She was delighted when I was hunting, as it gave her an excuse to go to meets, and keep in contact with all her hunting friends. She also had a family talent for enjoying the hospitality, before and after meets!

In fact I have had some association with many of the subjects in this book, but others I came across in my travels reporting on hunting around the world. George Watson who emigrated from Ireland to Australia in 1850, I became interested in when I was reporting on the Melbourne and the Oakland Foxhounds in Australia. His brother John hunted the Meath Foxhounds, and is credited with drafting the rules of polo. In fact the first recorded game of polo was played in Watson's home county of Carlow in 1870, and Watson was a dual international representing both Britain and Ireland. Toni de la Bouillerie a member of the Codd racing family in County Wexford I met when I hunted with her pack in Noyant in France, and Nancy Penn Smith Hannum when I was writing about Mr. Stewart's Cheshire Hounds in Unionville, Pennsylvania.

I found that many of the 31 people that I profile were very modest about their achievements. All were blessed with exceptional talent, a number achieving National, International and Olympic recognition, while others although talented had the added burden in life to overcome serious setbacks through illness and injury to achieve their own personal ambitions.

Hunting played a part as their way of relaxation, away from the competition of life, or in other equestrian disciplines like eventing, showjumping, dressage, racing, polo, hunter trials, showing or team chasing. But as I was reminded recently hunting is not a competition, so everybody is a winner That's what makes it different, that's why it is so much fun, and generates great stories. Some say that it is the equivalent to the excitement that a golfer would get if he was to score a hole in one every day!

Many made a life's work of horse riding, competing and dealing in horses, and particularly the Irish riders who promoted the unique qualities of the Irish horse around the world. Certainly a life riding and enjoying the outdoor life with horses was never on the Career Guidance Councillor's list of careers in school. Some of the people have been written about before, some not, but I wanted to tell my version of their story.

I would like to thank my wife Emer for her patience and assistance in proofing the manuscript of the book, and to two others that assisted me, my good friends Dick Cahill and Trevor Boate who both admit that they now know a little more about horses, and appreciate the bravery of riders more than when they first read the book. My daughter Sheila and my son Philip were also generous with their opinions.

I would also like to thank the editors of *The Irish Field*, Leo Powell and Siobhan English, who publish the popular weekly equestrian publication in Ireland, and the former editor Grania Willis who became the first Irishwoman to climb the North Face of Mount Everest who I am delighted to feature in my book. I have had the pleasure of contributing my hunting reports and features to the paper for a number of years.

So readers, I hope you enjoy this snapshot of the 31 equestrian personalities that I have chosen to write about, as much as I have enjoyed sketching out some of the amusing incidents and high points in their exciting lives.

Noel Mullins

Lady Molly Cusack-Smith

Lady Molly Cusack-Smith was the first lady master and huntsman of the famous Galway Blazer Foxhounds when she was appointed in 1939. She was also a talented clothes designer, cook and trained singer. She has often been described as having a sharp wit, and did not suffer fools gladly.

She formed her own hunt pack, the Bermingham and North Galway Foxhounds in 1943, having been loaned the northern part of the Blazer's hunt country.

Her hunt balls held in her home Bermingham House were legendary, and have given rise to many amusing stories over the years.

As a creative person, she enjoyed the company of friends in the art world like Augustus John, some of whose works are hanging in the Tate Gallery in London.

Lady Molly Cusack-Smith's personality certainly brightened up the West of Ireland for three quarters of a century, with her wit, her parties, and for the determination that she displayed when establishing herself as the first lady to hunt the Galway Blazer Foxhounds.

Many quotes are attributed to her which she never denied, such as one that was published in a prominent London Newspaper. After a hunt in Athenry, she asked a young man to hold her horse while she dismounted. He remarked that her horse was sweating up badly. She replied,

"Young man, if you were between my legs for five hours you would be sweating too". She grew up in a man's world, and was once described as having a sharp wit, and did not suffer fools gladly. But another side to her was

4

her genuine kindness to less well off people in the area. She also had a special relationship with her staff, and many remained working for her all their working lives.

Molly O'Rorke (her maiden name) was born in Dublin but lived most of her life in Bermingham House outside Tuam in north County Galway. Horses and hunting were a way of life from an early age as her father Charlie O'Rorke kenneled a pack of harriers on the estate, which she hunted on her pony.

Living Abroad

After her early schooling in Ireland she furthered her education in Sherburg School in England and then Paris where her mother spent a lot of time. Now living in the fashion capital of the world, she started a dressmaking business with a Russian friend. Although establishing herself in the world of haut couture, she decided later to go to live in London. Party time and the attraction of hunting on her favorite hunter Beau Geste with the fashionable packs like the Meynell and the Pytchley proved too attractive.

Master of the Galway Blazers

However in 1939 her love of foxhunting drew her back to County Galway where she was to become the first lady to hunt the famous Galway Blazers as Miss A M O'Rorke, exactly 100 years after her ancestor John Dennis, who was the first huntsman of the Galway Blazers. Preparing for her appointment as master and huntsman, she had spent the previous Summer practicing the correct calls on the hunting horn every hour, something she was to be very particular about when later employing huntsmen for her own private pack. A proud moment for her was parading the Blazer Foxhounds in the Royal Dublin Society Horse Show which was quite an achievement in such a short space of time with her new pack. But she had always a passion for hounds, horses she considered were only a way of getting through the country to keep in contact when hounds were hunting

During her mastership the Blazers hunting country was practically the whole of the County Galway, so she used to keep hounds in both the Blazer Kennels or in her own kennels at the home estate of Bermingham House in Tuam, depending on which part of the country she was hunting. It was quite common to use the train network to transport hounds and horses to meets on what were known as hunt specials, with the train times advertised on the hunt cards to accommodate followers and their horses but especially visitors, and it was often midnight when she arrived home in the kennels after a hard day's hunting.

The Bermingham and North Galway Foxhounds

In 1943 after four seasons the Blazers loaned her the northern part of their hunting country along Lough Corrib to the southern part of County Mayo and west of Roscommon so that she could form her own pack. It contained some of the best stone wall country numbering about 30 walls to the mile which was exciting for her followers. She kenneled her pack at her home Bermingham House. This had the advantage of a more manageable area for getting to and from meets. She had a yard full of hirelings for her house guests, who had the option of hunting with Lady Molly's own pack on Sundays and Wednesdays, or Tuesdays with the Blazers. She is remembered for having occasional transport problems. One day the hound trailer was towed by a Rolls Royce and another day by an itinerants van, but she did not care as long as she got to the meet. Her daughter Oonagh Mary joined her as a teenager as whipper in and then as joint master.

One memorable hunt was when hounds found a fox in Castlehacket and ran him to Annaghdown over a period of two hours. When the fox swam out to an island on Lough Corrib to safety only eight followers were at the finish at the lake shore.

Both her husband Sir Dermot and herself took on the joint mastership of the Westmeath Foxhounds, before Sir Dermot went as joint master to the Shillelagh Foxhounds in County Wicklow. Hunting falls eventually took their toll on her, as she broke nearly every bone in her body from falls off horses, but for some reason she never broke her collar bone which is usually one of the first bones for riders to break. She had a long and successfull mastership of her own pack, serving from 1946 to 1984, and many of those years she also hunted hounds.

Socialite

In her early days after living in Paris and London and coming back to Ireland she regularly socialised in Dublin with her friends in the art and fashion world often dining in what was then Ireland's best known, Jammets Restaurant. It was owned by French-born Louis and Yvonne Jammet, the latter of whom was a talented landscape artist, and sculptor, and a member of the White Stag Group. Her friends included stained glass artist Evie Hone, journalist Patrick Campbell, the Guinness heirs Gareth Oranmore and Browne and Desmond Guinness. She was also friends with many artists including the Welsh portrait artist and muralist Agustus John, who was the official World War 1 artist attached to the Canadian Corps. Many of his works are hanging in the Tate Gallery in London. John had a habit of doodling sketches on the table napkins over dinner. Thinking back Molly often regretted that she did not save the sketches as they would become very valuable and would have more than financed her to live the lifestyle she had been accustomed to. When running her home as a guest house it became a favorite haunt for Irish and overseas hunting parties, and artistic society. One night a visitor referred to her at dinner as a West Brit, and she picked up a plate and cracked it over his head. The following year at the Irish Master of Foxhounds Hound Show in the RDS in Dublin Hugh Robards who was master and huntsman of the County Limerick Foxhounds handed her a piece of a plate saying" I think Molly this belongs to you", much to her amusement! American Sherman Ruttle later joined her as joint master. When asked how he liked staying at Bermingham House, he replied that the secret of staying with Lady Molly was, "You got to learn to roll with the punches". In the early days everything was done on a grand scale with two maids, a butler, a cook, and outside a head man for the stables, a gardener and a kennelman, as well as several farmhands.

Many nationalities stayed in Bermingham House, either for hunting or while attending the Galway Races. Rolling Stones lead singer Mick Jagger and Marianne Faithfull took the house for a brief time. Some members of The Chieftans also visited as guests, and would sometimes play their unique arrangements of Irish music at her private parties, as did De Dannan. Molly liked to sing as she had a fine voice from her opera training in France. Her favorite songs were The Queen of Connemara and the West Awake. But there was a practical side to her as she made all her own clothes and curtains and furnishings for the house. She was totally independent and outspoken, knowing exactly what she wanted, and where she was going.

Molly's Hunt Balls were famous, and well sold out from year to year. Her gilt edged personal invitations were prized possessions, with many guests delighted to have the opportunity to meet the real lady, and not a bit put out at the possibility of being abused verbally by her. All would be taken in the spirit that was intended. The house lent itself to entertaining on a grand scale with paintings of her ancestors adorning the walls of the large entrance hall and dining rooms. Amongst the paintings is one of her husband Sir Dermot Cusack-Smith on his favorite horse, and another of Mollys favorite hound Planter. A smaller painting of Molly hangs on the wall of the main diningroom which was commissioned by Lady James Nelson. It features Molly in her red hunting livery sitting on a bar stool in Brendan Higgins Bar, the venue of the Blazers annual opening meet in Athenry. It was painted by portrait painter of Presidents and Church leaders Simon Coleman RHA.

As Molly was ill in her latter years, her daughter Oonagh Mary felt that in consideration of her poor health she should cancel the Hunt Ball. Molly would not hear of it, and told her that it was obvious that she was going to die anyway, and if she passed away during the ball that it would be perfectly acceptable to her, to close her bedroom door and turn the ball into a funeral wake for her friends! She was to die 2 years later in 1997 at 92 years of age. Some years before she died, Canon Corbett her local Church of Ireland Rector noticed that she was attending services in the Roman Catholic Church. When he pointed this out to her, and asked her when she intended to come back to her own church services she remarked, "When you stop singing those mournful hymns"!

Her hunting legacy lives on in her daughter Oonagh Mary who was joint master with her, and her grandaughter Joanne who also continues with a passion for hunting. Lady Molly Cusack-Smith could be kind or could be caustic, but she was also extremely popular as well as independent, and is certainly remembered by all those who came in contact with her. But she had many admirers who appreciated her achievements and her remarkable ability to make her mark on what was then very much a male dominated world.

The Author on the Lassie film set.

Grania Willis

Equestrian Journalist Grania Willis is the first Irishwoman to successfully climb the North Face of the highest mountain in the world Mount Everest.

As a result of a number of serious falls while hunting and eventing, she was advised on a number of occasions after surgery by her medical consultants to give up riding horses, as another serious fall could prove to be fatal.

She finally accepted rather reluctantly that her riding days were over, and not being a comfortable spectator she searched for a replacement sport to fill the vacuum. Her medical advisors were astonished that Grania's idea of a replacement sport was mountain climbing, an even more dangerous sport than riding horses.

In June 2005 Grania stood proudly on the summit of Mount Everest with her sherpa Karsang, defying medical advice, and proving that although she is by her own admission an ordinary woman, she is also an extraordinary woman.

Equestrian journalist Grania Willis is the first Irish woman to successfully summit the north face of the highest mountain in the world Mount Everest. After a number of accidents pursuing competitive eventing, showjumping and hunting, her medical advisers suggested that she give up her dangerous sports, as another fall could prove fatal. In an amazing change of direction of past times, instead of adopting a life as a sports spectator, she turned instead to an even more dangerous sport that of mountain climbing, which took her in June 2005 to the top of the world.

Background

Her father Jerome and mother Dilys were associated with the theatre and films, and met at the Royal Shakespeare Theatre in Statford upon Avon. Life with horses began for Grania when she learnt to ride as a child at riding schools in London and Surrey, before getting her first pony, Christopher Robin, and with her friends she used to gallop around Effingham Common in Surrey over a course made with parking cones that were 'borrowed' from the local police. She studied English Archaeology, and Greek and Roman drama at Lancaster University where she got her first opportunity to compete internationally in France and Germany for her University.

On graduation, and not yet sure what career to pursue, one of her favorite radio programs was Alister Cooke's 'Letters from America', and that started her interest in journalism. Fortunately she was offered a job as secretary to the editor of *Country Life*, which quickly led to a position as journalist for *Horse and Hound*. Her dilemma was answered, with a job that provided time for her passion for horses and her love of writing. A guiding light was to step in again, when during a job assignment to Ireland she was offered the position in 1980 as Editor of the Sports Horse section of *The Irish Field*.

Competitive Spirit

Her work was exciting being in contact with people in the Irish sports horse industry, reporting on horse sales, breeding and hunting, as well as affording her the opportunity to hunt with a huge number of packs all around Ireland. She also competed in eventing, showjumping and dressage competitions on a succession of horses, the most talented of which was Jailbird, a gelding she rode at international level, and was aiming for the top in three-day eventing until injury forced his permanent retirement. But, despite this and other disappointments, Grania is convinced that her competition career, and her experiences in the hunting field were instrumental in honing the determination that would eventually take her to the top of Everest. Always one to push herself to the limit, and fit from regular gym work and swimming, she decided to test her body and run the Dublin Marathon in 1989, and even though she had never run further than six miles in training, completed it in fractionally over four hours. She was not happy with the time and felt that she could have done much better, if she had more experience of racing pace. But three months later when reporting on a hunt in County Clare she had a serious fall, fracturing the base of her spine and causing disc damage in the lumber region, which required surgery and a lengthy stay in hospital.

But the hunting fall was actually Grania's second serious accident. Fifteen years earlier she had suffered near fatal injuries when rupturing her spleen and liver in a show jumping fall.

As a pupil of former European showjumping champion Iris Kellett, and by now competing regularly on the circuit, she leased on behalf of *The Irish Field*, one of Iris's home-bred horses Muse Light. Disaster struck during an indoor show at Kelletts when the horse fell during the second round and accidentally stood on Grania, resulting in serious abdominal injuries. Professor Paddy Collins in Jervis Street Hospital operated on her, opening her up from her breast bone to her pubic bone to save her life. He advised her that she was to drink no alcohol for six months, and no riding of horses, or men either! She was plagued by food allergies, resulting in cramps and nausea and putting her in danger of osteoporosis, but with good medical advise got the allergies resolved.

Her back problems came back in the early 1990's when she started riding and competing again. In 1993 when reporting from Badminton three day event her back went into spasm, and shortly afterwards while reporting on Punchestown three day event, her back locked from the neck down, necessitating a second bout of surgery. Reluctantly Grania had to face reality and make a heartbreaking decisions, to give up riding and competing, as another fall could be fatal. Her decision was further endorsed when two good friends of hers, international event riders David Foster and Sam Moore were killed while competing.

Filling the Competitive Vacuum

The decision to give up riding left a huge vacuum in Grania's life, but little did she know that 12 years later she would be the first Irishwoman to climb the north face of the world's highest mountain.

The start of the search for an equivalent adrenaline rush to replace cross-country riding was to begin with a 100km fundraising walk in Pokhara, Nepal in 2001 to raise money for Temple Street Children's Hospital. Although usually fit from riding and gym work, she set about hill walking in the Wicklow Hills in preparation. The plan was put on hold because of the September 11th attacks in America, and the massacre of the Nepalese Royal Family in Kathmandu. But the charity trip went ahead the following March, and a helicopter trip to Annapurna base camp started Grania's love affair with the mountains. This was further strengthened when on a flight with Buddha Air the pilot invited her into the cockpit to give her a full view of Mount Everest. She was stunned by the view. But she was aware that this time it was easy, partying now on St. Patrick's Day in Nepal and having fun. As friends became aware of her newfound love, birthday and Christmas gifts were all to do with the mountains. One present that struck a cord was a book 'Facing Up' written by the then youngest Briton to climb Everest, 23 year old Bear Gryll who had broken his back two years earlier free fall parachuting.

2003 was the 50th anniversary of the first climbers to summit Everest, Sir Edmund Hillary and Tenzing Norgay, which meant that there was a lot of activity on the mountain, but Grania had another opportunity to travel to Nepal on a support trek to meet an Irish team led by successful 1995 north face summitter Pat Falvey. One of Pat's expedition members was Dr. Clare O'Leary, who was forced to turn back due to gastroenteritis on her first attempt to conquer Everest, but she succeeded the following year, again from the southern route. Grania was now getting familiar with the local place names like Lukla, Phakding, Thadokski, Namche Bazarr, Sagamatha Park and the Dudh Koshi and Thadokshi rivers. She began to understand the dangers of altitude sickness and the threat of pulmonary and cerebral oedema. There were reminders of the dangers all around, like the memorial to sherpa Babu Chirri who held the record for the fastest accent of Everest, and for surviving for 21 hours without oxygen on the summit, only to be killed in 2001, and the news that day of another fatality when a porter was killed. Another reminder of the danger on the mountain was when Grania left her tent at night in the dark at base camp and slipped, only to be stopped by a large rock.

Financing of her Everest bid was solved when in 1993 her employer *The Irish Times* were restructuring, and also selling off *The Irish Field* which presented an opportunity to accept voluntary redundancy. Her work colleague Ann McLoone encouraged her further by telling her to take the money and go climb that mountain. So she took the money and, on Friday the 13th of February, 2004, she started her new climbing career in Dalkey Quarry with Jane Carney. She continued her training with Christopher Stacey on mountain skills, map reading and compass use, and climbing with the Irish Mountaineering Club. This was complemented by ice climbing practice on an 18 metre ice wall in a giant freezer in Kinlochleven in Scotland. In early 2004 she climbed Ben Nevis in Scotland nearly reaching the top when the weather turned. Next in the build up was climbing the 6,400 metre Mera Peak, and the 6,200 metre Island Peak on real Himalayan ice, all part of the time learning curve towards Everest. After a spell in the French and Italian Alps with Robbie Fenlon and former Royal Dublin Society chief executive Shane Cleary, she was ready now to take on bigger things and set her sights on 8,201 metre Cho Oyu, the world's sixth highest mountain. Reporting on the Athens Olympics and Dublin Horse Show interrupted her training, but she left for Tibet two days after the Games to join with Russell Brice's Himalayan Experience team. She reached the summit, but the levels of exhaustion made her question her readiness for Everest, especially as Russell told her that Everest was half as tough again, and twice as painful. However she had created her own record as the first Irishwoman to summit Cho Oyu.

Two days after her return from Tibet, the positive dope test on Irish Olympic gold medalist Cian O'Connor's horse Waterford Crystal caused a flurry of media interest, and the constant interviews on radio and TV affected her preparation for the Everest climb, but her determination never wavered.

But Grania's 2005 Everest expedition was so nearly called off when, on February 26, her 19 year old nephew Joe collapsed and died from a heart attack while out running. It was a tragic blow for the close knit family, but afterwards Grania became even more determined to go ahead with the Everest climb and dedicate it to Joe, and at the same time donate all the funds to two nominated charities, The Irish Hospice Foundation and St. Luke's Cancer Hospital. Back in training she tore her hamstring while ice climbing in Scotland, forcing her to stop training for five weeks. Daily physiotherapy and rehabilitation in the swimming pool, running against a resistance belt, got her back into the swing of things, and she also spent time at Peak Centre Ireland in Dublin, using a Go2 Altitude machine to get her body used to the reduced oxygen levels that she would meet on the mountain.

Focus on Everest

After a farewell party in a well-known Dublin hostelry Scruffy Murphys, Grania left Dublin at the end of March, thinking on the flight to Kathmandu how ironic it was that 12 years earlier she had come to terms with the medical advice to give up competitive riding, and was now in the final countdown for a bid to climb the highest mountain in the world! But it was no longer a practice exercise, this was the real thing, and she was going to be calling on all the mountaineering skills that she had gathered in the previous 12 months. This was it, the ultimate goal, dangerous, life threatening, body debilitating, but if she was accepted by Everest it was the chance to see the culmination of all her hard work. It would ensure her name would enter the history books, but that was not important to her, what was important was raising badly needed funds for the two charities and commemorating her recently deceased nephew Joe.

Arriving in the Hotel Tibet in Lhasa she was delighted to renew acquaintances with many of the climbers that were on the Cho Oyu expedition. As well as climbing, she was now also reporting on her HP iPAQ for *The Irish Times*. The weather was terrible, with cold winds and whirling dust storms. A reminder again of the dangers were all around, as members of a Korean expedition were there to try to recover the bodies of three of their colleagues who had died the previous year.

In a bid to acclimatise to the new altitude, the expedition members climbed the scree slopes that surrounded base camp, where it was so cold that clothes froze as they were washed. Meanwhile sherpas cut platforms for Camp

2 and 3. Up to 10km of rope was brought in and taken up the mountain by the sherpa team. Water was sourced by chopping ice and melting it. Temperatures were frequently well below -20 degrees Centigrade. Altitude sickness was already affecting some of the team, and Grania herself was suffering from a swollen face, and others from snow blindness. But the weather too was changing on the North Col with 80-100 km winds. News of fatalities on the south side were coming through when a Canadian climber got a heart attack and died, and an American guide fell into a crevasse and also died.

The window of the 21 - 22 May looked in doubt, but more disappointment came when Russell told them that he could not guarantee the climb would take place as the temperatures would be -30 degrees centigrade, with 60 km winds which was too dangerous. They were reminded of similar conditions in 1996 when 15 climbers died on one night.

Meanwhile a Slovenian climber who had reached the summit died on the way down from lack of oxygen. Another Bhutanese climber who lay dying fortunately found an oxygen bottle beside a dead Korean climber which saved his life. It was reported that an Indian Air Force officer succeeded in reaching the top, only to fall and die on the way down. It was a stark reminder that when you summit Everest that it is only half the job done, as you have to get down safely, and that the decent has claimed most lives. There are 27 bodies above High Camp 4 of whom four are easily visible.

Grania was assigned sherpa Karsang, a son of Ang Rita who had summitted Everest 10 times, and Karsang has already been to the top six times. Now Russell had advised them that there was another weather window, 4 -5 June, and that they were going ahead, but reminded them that there was no possibility of rescue, so if anybody ran into difficulties they would die. Word came through of the extremely windy conditions at 7,900 metres on Camp 3, and store tents were badly damaged. It was essential now to keep nourishment up, and sleeping would necessitate using oxygen.

On the 3rd of June they set off into a gale towards Camp 3, sapping stamina, the rock and ice climbing experience in Scotland was paying off, but it was heartbreaking meeting a couple who had to turn back within 40 metres of summitting. Reaching the camp at 7,900 metres it was important to rest and conserve energy.

At High Camp she was meeting more people who hadn't made it, as they were suffering from impaired vision and frostbite. Continuing the climb she reached 8,300 metre camp where she would rest until 11.00 p.m. that night, when the quest to climb the last 548 metres would begin. Just below was the body of George Mallory who died 75 years before. It is not known if he and his climbing partner Andrew Irvine reached the summit.

The emphasis now was to rehydrate fast and get food intake up. It was important to avoid the risk of frostbite by warming both hands and feet before going out, and putting crampons on inside tent, normally a cardinal sin in the mountaineering world. They set off in dark rocky terrain with oxygen masks on, heading for the Exit Cracks where lies the body only known as Green Boots because it is the only part of the body visible. There was real climbing difficulty finding footholds, but the terrain levelled out on reaching the First Step. The snow was falling heavier and getting colder, with 5 hours climbing to go. Disappointment set in when one of her fellow climbers gave up exhausted, compounded by the news on the radio that a German climber had just died. After the exertions of the Second Step, the terrain flattened out until the Third Step and it was just above here that she came across the body of the Slovenian climber Marco that she had met at Base Camp. Passing within feet of the corpse in worsening visibility, she tried to keep an eye on her sherpa Karsang who was setting the pace for Grania. Time was of the essence, and he felt that she was slowing down. There was still the tortuously long snow slope to labour up, and then the last narrow traverse above the North Face before the scramble up the final rocky outcrop. Checking how long more she had to climb with Karsang she was relieved when he said about 10 minutes. She was totally exhausted on the final 200 metre climb but delighted to be getting closer to the highest point in the world. Getting within view, she could see the Tibetan prayer flags fluttering in the wind as she inched her way to the final few exposed metres to the summit. She could also see two other people, the one-armed Australian climber Paul Hockey and his sherpa Nima.

As she hauled herself up the final steps to the summit, she suddenly realised that she had succeeded, she reached the roof of the world, and the spirit of her nephew Joe had been with her every step of the way. It was a hugely emotional moment, but the bad weather meant that there was no view, so she spent just 15 special minutes on the summit, took a couple of pictures, and then started on the long descent back down the mountain.

Grania was expecting the down-climb of the vertical rock face that was the Second Step would be the toughest part of the decent, and it certainly was spectacularly nerve-wracking, knowing that a slip here would be fatal. But there was far worse to come, as Grania ran out of oxygen at about 8,100 meters while still in the area known as the Death Zone. She was totally on her own, having sent her sherpa on ahead of her, and her radio batteries had died in the freezing temperatures, so she had no means of calling for help. Falling constantly, she was increasingly unable to keep going, and only the timely intervention of her sherpa, who reappeared with a fresh oxygen bottle, saved her life.

Grania insists that she is just an ordinary person who has been on an extraordinary journey. She gives inspiring talks on the climb to young schoolchildren, to clubs and associations, and to the goal-driven employees of many multinational companies. She leaves her audiences humbled, but inspired to focus on achieving whatever their personal goals are.

When asked would she go back and climb Mount Everest again, the answer was an unequivocal yes, but this time traversing the mountain by climbing the South face and descending by the North Face. What would her doctors think!

Finbar Ryan with the Galway Blazers

Elsie Morgan

Elsie Morgan was an exceptional horsewoman and had a natural affinity with a pack of foxhounds. She was born in Wales, and as a 12 year old she was already whipping in to the Llangibby Foxhounds.

She fell in love with west Waterford on a hunting visit to Ireland after the war, and went on to hunt the local pack for 31 seasons. Both herself and her husband Tom an international showjumping course designer became lifelong friends with the American master and huntsman Isaac Bell, and the person best known for developing the modern foxhound. He was then living in Lismore, County Waterford and together they developed a pack of hounds that were famous for their fox sense and distinctive white colour.

Elsie was also a producer and rider of top class showjumping horses, amongst them horses that competed for Italy at Olympic and Nations Cup level. As a rider she represented Ireland in the Nations Cup in Rotterdam and Ostend, as well as winning over 150 races including the European Derby at Boitsfort in Belgium.

Elsie Morgan

Although Elsie Morgan was born after the turn of the last century, she enjoys reminiscing about her life with horses and hounds. She is best known as the master and huntsman of the West Waterford Foxhounds, and of course for her white hounds that were bred especially for the hunt country. The author and former master and huntsman of the Galway Blazers, the Kilkennys and the South and West Wilts, and the person accredited as the inspiration for the modern hound, Isaac 'Ikey' Bell said of Elsie, "After watching you hunt hounds in the field, I don't know how I had the temerity to write a book on hunting". He recognised that Elsie Morgan was a natural talent with a pack of hounds. But she was also a successful International showjumper, race rider, breeder and producer of show horses and showjumpers.

Early days in Wales

She can recall her interest in hunting with her father Adolphus from the age of three, riding her pony Little Tom who was a prolific prize winner taking a class at the Royal Dublin Society. As a 12 year old she was already whipping in to the Llangibby Foxhounds huntsman Pat Thatcher son of the famous Leicestershire huntsman Arthur Thatcher. Her father died when she was 17 years old so she had to run the family farm on her own as well as whipping in twice a week. They hunted around Monmouthshire and Gwent. On the weekends she was proving to be one of the best point to point riders in the country riding her first winner as a 14 year old, and became known as the 'Queen of the Flappers', winning over 100 flapper races.

Hunting, Racing and Showjumping on the Continent

Her husband Captain Tom Morgan. first met her when he was home on leave during the Second World War. He remembers that she was with a friend and was riding a beautiful bay mare. He fell in love immediately with both Elsie Preston and her bay mare. The next time home on leave he proposed to her and they got married. He was then stationed in Germany after the war in 1946, and when Elsie was coming out to join him he asked her to take out the bay mare and some hounds. Elsie drafted $4^1/_2$ couple from the Llangibby, and they formed a Garrison Pack with the members well turned out in their red hunting coats. Foxes were scarce, but they had great fun hunting roe deer that were plentiful around Schleswig Holstein, accounting for regular runs of 10-12 miles over good double bank and gorse country close to the sea. During that time she was also race riding in Belgium winning the Derby des Dames in Brussels, and the Grand Prix des Dames d'Ostende, as well as riding on the B.O.A.R Showjumping Team.

West Waterford Hounds

In 1949 Elsie and Tom came on holidays to West Waterford to see an army friend Brian Pierce. They had a day's hunting with the master Major Bill Scott resulting in Elsie whipping into Major Anthony Burke who was hunting the hounds. On Major Burke's departure Elsie took over hunting the pack in 1953 which was to last for 31 seasons of top drawer hunting, and a friendship between Tom and herself and Isaac Bell. They developed a hound breeding policy that produced a pack of hounds that was to draw the attention of the real hound breeders of the hunting world. They had numerous requests for drafts of their West Waterford hounds by packs in Ireland, England and particularly in America. Even Ben Hardaway who is the best known American master of hounds, hunting his Midland Hounds in Georgia visited the Morgans frequently. Hardaway has over 200 hounds in his kennels, and he has spent his life trying to breed the perfect hound. He was so impressed with the West Waterford hounds that he has drafted many of their hounds to his pack, particularly progeny from Gladstone the son of College Valley Legion '49 and Cumberland Guilty '48 by Blencathra Mountain that Bell referred to as ugly, but a beautiful machine. Also the progeny of Pytchely Crafty '54 that was successfully crossed with Fell lines. Hardaway now has 30 to 40 lines going back to those famous West Waterford hounds. Isaac Bell had retired because of arthritis in his hips to Lismore beside the Morgan's farm in Waterford, having hunted three different packs for a total of 27 seasons. A member of a wealthy American family that owned the Chicago Times, he was at Harrow with Winston Churchill and he dedicated his life to hunting hounds and breaking with tradition in developing what is now known as the modern foxhound, where he crossed English with Welsh and Fell hounds. Meeting the Morgans was like a new lease of life for him, and he was so impressed with Elsie's skill with hounds that he promised to breed her "a pack worthy of her talents", saying that it could take 10 years to breed the right pack for the country. He built them a new kennels on their newly acquired farm, and set about sourcing hounds from his friends the Duke of Beaufort and Masters of the Pytchley, and the College Valley. He line bred the best foxhounds that he had seen hunting. The pack were so close bred that only four College Valley stallion hounds were used. They were predominately white in color so that they could be easily seen in the mountainous country, but had the drive, nose, cry and independence so that they could hold the line of a fox regardless how difficult the terrain or scenting conditions were without any assistance. The pack was described by one observer from a meet at Millstreet when they were scaling the Knockmealdown Mountains, hard on the brush of their fox, that they were like a flock of seagulls flying across the mountain.

Elsie was a superb horsewoman, already a Grand Prix showjumping rider having jumped in two Nations Cups for Ireland, and showed that she could cross the hunting country with ease. One day on a terrific run of over 14 miles she came to a gate that was all wired up front and back, with no apparent way to jump into the next paddock. In order to keep with her hounds Elsie pointed her horse at the two feet square topped stone pillar, six feet in height, and asked her horse to bank it. He responded by scaling the height and accurately placing his four feet on top of the pillar while he pushed off with his hind legs and safely landed in the next field.. Needless to say nobody followed. Another day they decided to have a day with their friend Thady Ryan and his Scarteen Hounds at Limerick Junction. Hounds found immediately at the first draw at Ballykisteen Stud, and within minutes were two fields ahead when at the back of the village of Oola they crossed the road with Elsie out front and Pat Hogan right behind them. Pat remarked turning up his collar that it was a great day for a swim. As they galloped across the field he wheeled right while Elsie went straight ahead riding the line of the fox. Thady and the field turned back to look for another way out over the bridge as the river was in flood. Whipper in Tommy Dwyer had fallen into the river, but Elsie took the 18 foot wide river on and jumped it bank to bank onto a landing three feet higher than take off. Pat Hogan swam the river with his horse and got out further down at a low bank which was a drinking place for cattle.

On another occasion Thady Ryan invited her to take some of her hounds to a meet at Derk House and hunt them with his Scarteen 'Black and Tan' Hounds. On the way up the avenue one of Elsie's bitches Gladstone put her front feet up on a lime tree and looked up and babbled in the direction of a bed of twigs in the upper bough where it appeared as if a fox was hiding. Thady asked Elsie "Can you trust her". Elsie replied "With my life". They left the fox and came back later after drawing a few other coverts. When they returned with hounds to the lime tree, they kept the pack back for about 10 minutes to allow the fox to get away. The fox jumped down from the lime tree and away, but with poor scent they eventually lost him. About 4.00 p.m. as it got colder both packs were taken to draw the back of the creamery above Pallasgreen. They immediately found and were away. Elsie was first to the road before the hounds, watching the line all the time and blew them on, which was easy as her white hounds were out in front, running hard competing with each other and the Scarteen pack. All the followers could see was a stream of white hounds followed by a similar stream of black and tans with one rider behind them, Elsie Morgan. As they pushed their fox over the Sugarloaf Hill she had to jump a 12 foot drop to get to the pack, and she could be heard blowing the fox to ground behind the village of Old Pallas. It was five minutes before other riders arrived. Only Thady Ryan, Pat Hogan, Tom and Kathy Ronan finished. Tommy Dwyer's horse collapsed with the relentless pace. Pat Hogan wanted to buy Elsie's horse, but her husband Tom said jokingly, "I do not consider him an exceptional horse, but adequate for exercising hounds in the West Waterford hunting country"! The point was 5 miles and 11 miles as they ran in 65 minutes over the stiffest of country, with only one check on the road. Tom Morgan remarked that the only other time he heard such music was from Ben Hardaway's Midland Hounds in Fitzpatrick Alabama, and the Berlin Philharmonic Orchestra playing Beethovan's 9th Symphony!

There was to follow an enjoyable period for Ikey, as he was able to hunt again, if only by car. If the scent was good even in the summer he would come up to the kennels in the evening and the three of them would take the hounds to the Duke of Devonshires Skirook Wood with Elsie and Tom mounted and Ikey marking point in his car driven by his nurse. He enjoyed the hilltopping, and would study closely which hounds were doing best. Elsie describes Ikey as Superman, with a one track mind, hunting and hounds. When he was master of the West Wilts he had 100 hunters stabled and 100 couple of hounds, and spent a lot of money supporting his sport.

Sadly the good times with Ikey came to an end when one night he invited Elsie and Tom to dinner, knowing that his life was close to the end. After dinner sitting in his wheelchair he took out his old silver hunting horn and blew 'Gone Away', before they left. They both cried in the car on the way home, and one of the greatest and most meticulous breeder of hounds the hunting world has ever known, passed away a few weeks later.

However they also had the company of another hunting enthusiast Bay de Coursey Parry who rented a house on their farm for two years while he was writing his autobiography. A former huntsman of the Cumberland Hounds he was well known as a hunting journalist writing regularly under the name of Dalesman for *Horse and Hound*.

Breeding and Producing Horses

Elsie's best horses were Finola and Rooney who was an International showjumper and she was invited by Colonel Jack Lewis to represent Ireland in the Nations Cup replacing Tommy Wade in Ostend in 1963, and again in Rotterdam with Frank McGarry as Chef d'Equippe. The master of Hickstead Douglas Bunn wanted to buy Rooney but Elsie would not sell him. He was by Ambassador and the dam was by Isaac Bell's stallion Laughtons Last that equine artist Lionel Edwards painted when Bell hunted hounds off him when master and huntsman of the Kilkenny Foxhounds. Occasionally showjumping rider Francie Kearns rode and qualified some of Elsie's horses. Rooney was a great all rounder, winning all around Ireland and at the RDS in Dublin. Tom had 17 happy seasons riding him two days a week as field master with only one fall. Elsie also produced a Middleweight Dublin Champion and three International showjumpers for Italy, Red Fox who won a Grand Prix in Rome ridden by Captain Piero D'Inzeo and Gone Away who represented Italy ridden by his brother Colonel Raimondo D'Inzeo, as well as Hill Fox who was on the Italian Olympic team in Munich.

During this time Elsie was riding winners in point to points, including a win on a chance ride Fitzcar in the Maiden Race at Dungarvin point to point. Tom and Elsie travelled frequently to shows around the country as Tom was an international course builder, and one of the highlights of his career was course building and judging hunters at Melbourne Show in Australia in 1974. Their travels also took them to America to fox hunt and to judge hounds at many of their national hound shows.

Having competed at Bandon Show for 45 years, Elsie presented the European Derby Cup that she won in the race riding Beaujolais at Boitsfort in Belgium. One of her opposing jockeys that day was Peter Scudamore's father.

Elsie Morgan retired as Master and huntsman of the West Waterford Foxhounds when she was 71 years of age having hunted the pack for 31 seasons. But recently she was invited back as joint master to assist in the breeding of the pack, and advising on running the hunt country, while Tom designed the new kennels and supervised the building work. She follows the West Waterford by car two days a week, and she often manages to include another day with a neighbouring pack.

Tara Harrier hounds

Tommy Brennan

Tommy Brennan is often referred to as the complete rider, having represented Ireland in both showjumping and eventing. He enjoyed jumping the wide ditches of County Meath following the hunt, winning a World Team Championship Three Day Event, and representing his country at the Olympic Games. In a relatively short showjumping career he won over 1,000 red rosettes, 55 International competitions and the Dublin Showjumping Championship on nine different horses.

He is a celebrated eventing course designer, having created imaginative courses all over Ireland, and internationally in Beijing in China, Doha in Qatar and Melbourne in Australia.

As a bloodstock agent and breeder, he has the ability to source a horse to suit a client that has plans to compete at the highest level, or a client that plans to ride for pleasure.

It is perhaps true to say, that most people in the horse industry would consider Tommy Brennan as probably the most complete and best all round rider in multiple equestrians disciplines that Ireland has produced. He hunted regularly, was a winning point to point rider when riding for Paddy Murphy a neighboring trainer in his home county of Kilkenny. He represented Ireland in eventing and showjumping, at International and Olympic level all around the world.

Now retired from riding, he is a respected bloodstock agent, having a good eye for a horse in the rough, and able to match a horse to a potential client whether their intention is just to ride for leisure or at representative level. He is also in demand as a show judge, and has bred some very good young horses, and above all as an Internationally recognised course designer.

Hunting

From a very young age Tommy followed the local hounds in his native County Kilkenny like the Kilmoganny Hounds where he held office as Honorary Secretary and Chairman for many years, and the Kilkenny Foxhounds when they were hunted by Major Victor McCalmont. Although he maintained his farm in the county, he was spending more time in Dublin and travelling in Continental Europe showjumping when he was riding for Omar Van Landeghen, probably the largest beef exporter at the time, who was shipping 75,000 cattle out of Ireland each year. He hunted all his showjumpers regardless of how valuable they were, with local packs such as the Fingal Harriers and the Ward Union Staghounds. He enjoyed hunting, as it was a great era with many of the well known hunting families like the Craigie, Collen, Duff, Mangan, Duffy, Ryan and Dreaper families who were very active in the hunt clubs. Racing went hand in hand with hunting, and he has many happy memories of riding alongside successfull owners like Standish Collen who owned National Hunt horses like Kilkilowen and Bold Flyer both trained by Jim Dreaper. Later Collen's daughter Sarah won the Galway Plate on Bold Flyer.

Tommy is a renowned storyteller, and very popular as a guest speaker at equestrian functions. Reminiscing on one of his most unusual hunting experiences, he immediately remembers a horse called Tarzan who he describes as 'almost unridable'. He was owned by Galway Blazers field master Willie Leahy who hired him out to visitors, but often clients would hand him back in the first field, when they were not able to manage him. Despite the fact that he 'pulled like a train', Tommy saw it as a challenge, and when hunting him one day decided to face him at the highest point of some of the biggest Galway double walls, and after hitting a few the horse began to have some manners. Derek Trench who was acting as field master was threatening to send him home, but Tommy insisted that the horse was almost impossible, and that Willie Leahy should be paying him to ride him, which according to Tommy was very unlikely. Later in the evening around Turloughmore he found himself facing up to what looked like a thatched roof of a house in the distance, similar to a wide root clamp roof that farmers in that area used to house vegetables and animal feed during the Winter. He put as he says 'his foot to boards' and faced Tarzan at this unusual obstacle that increased in size as they got closer, and clearing the thatched roof there was a huge drop on the landing side. As the horse touched down and Tommy picked him up, he looked back over his shoulder like a jockey, to discover he had cleared a country cottage and the lady of the house was leaning out over the half door in total shock, while at the same time he added, that she continued to breast feed her baby!

Course Designer
Tommy is probably best known now as a designer of cross country hunter trial and event courses, with a flair for design and sensitive to the historical culture of whatever country he is building in. One can see in Punchestown as far back as the 1991 European Championships, the sheer imagination in his course building that makes an event a more pleasurable experience for spectators, with solidly built fences always well presented. His plan was to create a heritage park type course with landmarks from each county in Ireland, but cost dictated that it be done on a reduced scale, but still he managed to include miniature replicas of many of the well known landmarks like the Round Tower of Glendalough and the Sally Gap in County Wicklow, and the Dolmen fence which has a top capping that weighs $12^{1}/_{2}$ tons. He also has included replicas of the old Crannog buildings of County Clare, and Newgrange, the site of the Winter Equinox Tomb in County Meath. He knows how to please fence sponsors too, with fences recently built like the Porsche Cayman Island and the Irish Sport Horse Gene Pool fences. At Tattersalls Sales Complex which hosts an annual Three Day Event he has reproduced a replica of the Ballingarry Coal Mine carriages, *The Irish Field* Ballistrade, and an Auctioneers Rostrum. At Milverton Estate he featured a Deer Cart which was appropriate as the event was hosted by the Ward Union Staghounds. His skills and imagination as a course builder have been recognised internationally too, especially when he was invited to design the course for the World Championships that was to be run in Ireland in 1998, but the sponsors pulled out and it moved to Rome. Before the cancellation he was offered the design of the Sydney Olympic course for 2000 but reluctantly turned it down as he felt he was committed to the World Championships in Ireland not knowing in advance that it was to be cancelled. He designed the Asia Pacific Games Course in Melbourne in 1995, and the first Three Day Event course in Beijing in China in 2003. Towards the end of 2006 he is designing the course for the Asian Games in Qatar. Having been the first designer to work in China on course design, he was the front runner to design the Three Day Event Course for the 2008 Olympics in China. But when it was moved to Hong Kong as a result of a change in sponsors, it was unfortunate for Tommy that the design was awarded to British course designers.

His course design for the Young Eventer Class in the Main Arena at the Royal Dublin Society in 2006 was considered by many as a masterpiece. One of the features was a combination, the first part being a spider carved in wood, with the second part an upright spiders web also constructed in wood that competitors had to jump through.

Three Day Eventing
He was selected for the Irish Olympic Team at Kariuzawa in Japan in 1964 riding Kilkenny, a horse that had already won six international showjumping competitions including wins in Aachen in Germany and Dublin. The horse was owned by Omar Van Landeghem of Skidoo Stud in North County Dublin. The rest of the team was made up of Tony Cameron on Black Salmon, who finished 5th, John Harty riding San Michele who was 18th, and Captain Harry Freeman Jackson on Saint Finbarr who was 28th. The team placings were Italy 1st, USA 2nd, and West Germany 3rd. Because of the long journey horses were standing for 57 hours and another 5 hour road journey to the stables. Kilkenny performed well being one of only twelve clear showjumping rounds out of thirty four. Ireland finished 4th in the team placings, only 13.7 points dividing them and a bronze medal. From a breeding point of view eight of the first eighteen horses were Irish bred, including all the Italian team horses who won the gold medal. Thady Ryan the former master of the Scarteen 'Black and Tan' Foxhounds was Chef d'Equipe.

In 1966 Tommy was selected for the Irish team for the first World Championships at Burghley. Because of an outbreak of equine flu no teams from the rest of Europe were allowed to travel, resulting in the lineup of Ireland, Britain, United States of America, Argentina and the U.S.S.R. Riding Kilkenny again, with Major Eddie Boylan on Durlas Eile, Penny Moreton on Loughlin and Virginia Freeman-Jackson on Sam Weller, Ireland had a remarkable competition and were crowned World team champions.

In the Mexico Olympics in Avandaro in 1968, Tommy was riding March Hawk owned by Mrs K.L. Kjaer, Penny Moreton on Loughlin owned by John Galvin, Diana Wilson on Chianti Rosso, and Juliet Jobling-Purser on Jenny. The team placings were Britain 1st, America 2nd and Australia 3rd. Horses arrived 30 days before the event to acclimatise them to the high altitude. Tommy was reserve rider in both showjumping and eventing, and when Alan Lillingston's horse Biddlecombe incurred a tendon injury, he was replaced by Tommy and March Hawk. Eddie Boylan's former European champion Durlas Eile by now was on the Canadian team and Tommy's horse Kilkenny was on the American team ridden by Jimmy Wofford who a won a silver team medal, and again at the Munich Olympics having been sold on in the meantime. Disaster struck for Ireland as Loughlin broke his back and had to be put down. There was a deluge of non stop rain and Diana Wilson just got through with three refusals. Tommy was to go second last, and by now the steeplechase course was starting to flood. As he started the cross country phase the flooding was extremely serious, with fence seven barely visible, and fence six nearly submerged. The horse through no fault of his own, caught the top of a fence which was by now under water and turned him over. The event should have been stopped and rescheduled as riders and horses were in danger of being drowned. Tommy and his horse at one point disappeared under water only for both to swim separately to dry ground. March Hawk could go no further and was eliminated. The officials got the weather forecast wrong and did not act when the course was in flood, and reschedule the steeplechase and cross country element.

Showjumping

Brennan had an even more illustrious career of 12 years in showjumping leaving a record that few could match. Most of his horses he produced himself, and schooled them from the time they were broken, taking them up the grades to top level competition. He has been associated with many top class horses in his career in showjumping, particularly the steel grey Ambassador. He was unfortunate in the lead up to the Munich Olympics in 1972, in not being allowed to compete with Ambassador as he was considered ineligible for the team. The reason given by the Federation was that Tommy was considered to be a professional, even though his occupation clearly stated that he was a farmer and bloodstock agent. Tommy won the case in Court but the Federation changed the rule again. The decision was deemed to be unfair by many, and the criteria were later changed, but not in time to allow him to travel. But Tommy's horse Ambassador did win an Olympic Gold medal that year when jumping for the Italian Team ridden by Graziana Mancinelli. He was also associated with other horses like Kilbride that he owned in partnership with Omar Van Landegham, who was a very progressive showjumping supporter, and generous owner. He was the first owner to charter an aircraft to take all his showjumpers on tour of the big shows in Frankfurt, Ostend and Rome, and would also take other riders like Leslie Fitzpatrick and Brian McNicholl without any subsidy from the Equestrian Federation of Ireland. Other horses that he rode were Westcourt and Abbeyville owned by former Taoiseach (Irish Prime Minister) Charles Haughey who was a regular hunt follower, particularly of the Ward Union Staghounds, but he also used to hunt with other packs around the country. Tommy considered Haughey an extremely lucky owner of horses, and he won numerous competitions on Haughey's horse Abbeyville by Nordlys. She was later named Miss Moet when purchased by Brazilian rider Nelson Pessoa, and went on to win a record number of 173 Puissance Competitions, all over the world. It was calculated that the mare jumped over 2 meters on 120 occasions, jumping 7 feet 8 inches with Pessoa. She was bred by Sammy O'Connell in County Waterford. Haughey refused a big offer for another of his good horses Feiltrim, but it allowed his daughter Eimear now a successful bloodstock breeder and Chairman of Goffs Bloodstock Sales to compete in two European Championships. Tommy produced and rode Loch an Easpaig in his early showjumping campaigns, and he was later to go on and compete for Ireland when ridden by the Irish Army rider Colonel Bill Ringrose. Another horse that Tommy produced to top level was Westcourt which was sold to the Italian rider Piero D'Inzeo.

Tommy Brennan's record in showjumping would be difficult to match, with over 1,000 red rosettes, and 55 international wins. In Dublin he won the showjumping championship on nine different horses, and was leading rider on many occasions as well as leading rider at the Rotterdam and Ostend Shows. In 1964 he won:

> The Dublin Horse Show Centenary Stakes on Donegal.
> The Sandymount Stakes again in Dublin on Kilkenny.
> Prix Henri Serruys in Ostend on Killane.
> Prix des Habits Rouge in Ostend on Kilrush.
> Prix d'Adieu in Ostend on Donegal.

Tommy won the Prix des Habits Rouge again in 1965 but on a different horse, named Donegal .

In the first Hickstead Derby he was runner up to another famous Irish showjumper Seamus Hayes riding Goodbye. One of the highest honors for an Irish rider is to be chosen for a Nations Cup Team particularly the competition held each August at the Royal Dublin Society show grounds in the center of Dublin city for the Aga Khan Cup. This was one of the few high level competition that eluded him, being on teams that were second on three different occasions.

Bloodstock Agent

He is renowned for his ability to find suitable horses for his many clients all over the world. An amusing incident happened when Queen Elizabeth expressed her interest in buying Kilkenny for her daughter Princess Anne who won a European Championship on her horse Doublet in Moscow. The owner Omar Van Landegham said "Tell her Majesty that she has not enough money to buy him"!

Brennan's hobbies are described in the publication *Who's Who in Ireland* as 'Anything equestrian, and interesting ladies', and he is quick to point out that having never married that he is still available and on the market!. But his friends say they doubt it, as Tommy has managed to 'Slip his headcollar' on a number of occasions, especially when it comes to being tied down! He continues to be a familiar face at all the major equine events in Ireland, particularly Punchestown and Tattersalls where he has left his mark on course design. Now achieving world attention for his unique creations of Three Day Event courses in Beijing, China, the Asia Pacific Games in Melbourne and the Asian Games in Qatar in the Gulf States, an Olympic Games course design commission is surely not out of the question.

Kildare Foxhounds masters l to r Charles O'Reilly and Rupert Macauley on Punchestown Racecourse

Florrie Webb

Florrie Webb gained a reputation as an accomplished horseman, as well as being master and huntsman of the Wicklow Foxhounds for 16 seasons.

What made him different was that he had a serious accident as a young man, when he caught his left arm in the power roll of a combine harvester resulting in it being severed below the elbow. For a brief period he wore an artificial hand, but he abandoned it as he found that when he had a fall off one of his horses that it was more dangerous and painful to fall on the solid artificial arm.

Despite having only the use of his right hand it did not deter him from leading a normal life riding horses, or winning on the racetrack.

Most riders find it a difficult enough challenge to ride with the aid of two hands, but John Florence 'Florrie' Webb did not have that choice, having lost his left arm just below the elbow as a result of an accident when in his 20's. Yet never one to let obstacles get in his way, his life has been centered around breaking, producing and riding young horses, point to point riding and as master and huntsman of the Wicklow Foxhounds.

Webb was born in Gorey, County Wexford, into a cattle and horse dealing family. His father Joe trained and hunted young horses, and one of Florries' proudest memories was sitting with his father as a young child in front of the saddle as they hacked into Crann Ford after a hunt with the Island Foxhounds. His mother passed away when he was only 8 years old. He never owned a pony, going straight into horses as soon as he was able to ride, and particularly remembering Willie Ward's good bay mare that he hunted regularly with the Island when Tom Fitzsimons who also hunted the Ward Union Staghounds, was huntsman. At school his favourite subject was 'mitching', or going absent from school, but when at school his ears would be pricked when he heard the sound of a horse coming up the road to the forge which was next door to the school. But he maintains the best University of life is time spent buying and selling at horse fairs, where you not only become a good judge of a horse, but also become an even better judge of people. He maintains he never made real money from horse dealing, but horse money was lucky money. In the Winter as soon as school was finished he would race out the road to where the hounds were hunting to catch a chance ride at the end of the day, or the opportunity to hack a horse home. With no tack shops in those days one had to improvise, so when hunting the ordinary flat cap was worn backwards so that it would reduce the chance of it blowing away. Childrens' saddles and jodhpurs were a rare item, so Webb used to cut the toes off long adult stockings and pull them over his knees to stop the stirrup leathers pinching his legs.

His life was to change after a freak accident in 1953, when his clothes got caught in the power drive of the combine harvester, severing his left arm completely below the elbow, and causing five breaks in the upper arm. Such was his determination that three weeks after he was released from hospital he was riding young horses again. Although he was fitted with an artificial arm and hand, he soon cast it aside after a fall from a horse caused him to land on the prosthesis which hurt him. Sometimes as a practical joke for people who did not know that he had an artificial left hand, he used to hammer nails into timber to their astonishment. Like the jockeys he used to tie a knot in the reins which made it easier to control a horse using one hand.

The reason he maintained that he had no difficulty riding his own horses is that he made all of them 'on the ground' before he sat on them regardless of how long it took, and because he was riding essentially with one hand he was careful in making a horse's mouth so that they could all be ridden in a plain snaffle bit. He went on to explain that before the volume of traffic increased on the roads, part of breaking a young horse was walking him for up to two hours a day all around the streets of the village of Gorey for at least six weeks, often resting for a chat with friends while his horse was encouraged to relax beside him. In this way they got accustomed to traffic and noise, and were easy to back after that. As he only used plain snaffle bits, he cannot understand why so many people are using three ring snaffles bits today, and the only conclusion that he can come to is that not enough time is given to the groundwork and mouthing before a horse is backed. As a rider Pam Chapman describes Florrie as "a good rider, with guts to burn, who would go anywhere on a horse". Despite dislocating his arm loading cattle and breaking his two legs when a horse slipped on the road, as soon as he felt he could ride and often against his doctor's advice, he was back in the saddle again. His explanation as to why horses from County Wexford are popular is first of all because Wexford people have an inbred interest in horses, and secondly they feed them well from an early age. He goes on to say that a horse bought in Wexford will be an even better horse when a person gets him home!

He won an Open Lightweight Race in the Island Point to Point fixture in Gorey riding his own horse Red Bar. Although he ran a dealing yard where horses were turned over quickly as soon as profit could be made on them, he was also successful in showing classes particularly with his grey mare Estrella by Marwood out of Spa Bridge that was produced by Pam Chapman and was Reserve Champion in the Mare Championship at the Royal Dublin Society Show in Dublin. The horse was sold to a client in Germany at a tidy profit. Another of his mares won her class and the Championship at Adamstown Show.

Foxhunting was always in his blood, as can be seen in the hallway of his house where the mask of a fox is hanging on the wall, that on the 21 November 1936 was found on Ballyhoose Hill and accounted for in Prospect with only his father Joe with the hounds at the end after a cracking run of more than an hour over challenging country. All of Florrie's seven children hunted, but his daughters Anita, Deirdre and Mary and his son Joseph were particularly keen, but they all have pursued other careers at home and abroad. Florrie kept and hunted the Gorey and District Beagles for 22 seasons, before handing over to his cousin Herbert Stephens. He was invited to hunt the Wicklow Foxhounds which he did for 15 seasons under masters Mrs. Henry Priest, Ian Martin and Richard Green, and shortly afterwards he was appointed master of the pack. At an opening meet at Arklow, at the end of the day he had to hack horses and hounds 10 miles on the road home to Gorey. He is quite modest about his own red letter days hunting hounds, and instead prefers to recount the best three days hunting in his lifetime, all with other packs. One was with the current huntsman of the Island Foxhounds Billy Connors, who he maintains is one of the best riders in the country. Hounds found at the far side of Salsboro, and put their fox to ground at the railway bank of Camolin. He describes the fox as a 'crooked little bugger', as he ran a twisty line which he says was a pleasure to watch. The next was with the Meath Foxhounds with Johnny Henry Snr. as huntsman at Doreys Forge. Only six finished including a clergyman complete with a white collar that Florrie describes as a 'hardy good buck' on a horse. The run was fast and long, and that night when he was driving home through the Phoenix Park in Dublin he noticed that his horse was very quiet, so when he checked he found him lying down asleep in the trailer he was so exhausted. The last of the trio of best hunts was with the Kilmoganny Harriers when Rory Dicker was huntsman. They got a run that he describes as like lightening, from Hugganstown near Mullinavat. The Mullinavat Harriers were another pack that he liked to hunt with especially when Larry Byrne was huntsman, as he was always sure of having some sport. He feels that because artificial fertilizer is being used in such large quantities today that scent is more difficult for hounds to keep a line, and accounts for many of the short runs compared with the old days that many packs are experiencing. One day a fox was marked to ground and Florrie went to have a look down the earth. When the fox snapped at his hand, Florrie was heard to say to the fox "Now, now, don't be like that, fingers are in short supply where I am concerned"! On another occasion when hunting hounds three visitors that he described as more suitably dressed for golf were pressing him all day. So he decided to find the widest drain, and having found one and safely cleared it himself, he looked back with delight at the sight of the three individuals and their horses with their heads scarcely visible trying to scramble out of the depths of it. He recalls buying a horse in Waterford that continuously fell out hunting. Despite being encouraged by his family to sell him on he persevered and he proudly states that once he got the horse to drop his eye and look at the fence that he could jump him "onto the fork of a tree".

Now over 80 years old, Florrie has two brood mares as he says, with a bit of bone, one by Walter Kent's horse Don Tristan that he particularly likes, and he is looking forward to seeing their foals on the ground. Aside from sourcing the occasional horse for other people, he is still trying to find a suitable horse for himself to hunt with the Island Foxhounds next season. Perhaps we will see the former huntsman and master of the Wicklow Foxhounds tackle the Wexford banks that he knows so well again in the near future.

Puppy in the Rosetree Hounds Kennels in America

John Huston

Film Director and Actor John Huston first visited Ireland in 1951 and discovered his passion for foxhunting and breeding bloodstock. He acquired St. Clerans Estate standing on over 100 acres outside the town of Loughrea in County Galway, and quickly set about renovating the buildings, and furnishing them with period furniture and art from his travels around the world.

In 1960 he was invited to become master of the Galway Blazers Foxhounds, and enjoyed ten of the happiest years of his life jumping the famous stone walls of Galway in between periods away filming screen classics like African Queen and Moby Dick.

He formed a Connemara Pony Stud and also produced show horses and thoroughbreds.

His home became a favorite location for entertaining well known personalities associated with the film industry, like Arthur Miller, Gregory Peck, Deborah Kerr, John Steinbeck, Burl Ives, Ursula Andress, Jean Paul Belmondo and Cary Grant.

Film Director and actor John Huston first visited Ireland in 1951 at the invitation of Lady Oonagh Oranmore and Browne, a member of the Guinness brewing family, which was also his first time to attend a Galway Blazers hunt ball. The ball at the Gresham Hotel in Dublin did not disappoint, as the night, or rather the early morning ended in high spirits accounting for an unusual number of casualties. Although he had hunted in America and Britain he liked the informality of hunting in Ireland, and decided to rent Courtown House in County Kildare. The staff that went to work for him, like his estate manager Betty O'Kelly and stud groom Paddy Lynch stayed with him for the duration of his time in Ireland. He used this base to hunt with many of the foxhound packs like the Meath, Kildare, Limerick Foxhounds and the Ward Union Staghounds. He liked the different natural obstacles like the stone walls of County Galway, the ditches of the County Meath and the Ward Union Staghounds, and the imposing double banks of County Limerick.

New Home in St. Clerans

On one of his hunting trips in the west of Ireland he discovered an old house, St. Clerans in need of repair, set on over 100 acres with a lovely old stone stable yard and a river flowing through it owned by the Land Commission. Situated between Loughrea and Athenry in County Galway what was even more interesting was that it was for sale, and could be probably purchased at a reasonable price. He was taken by the surroundings, and was successful in acquiring it at the auction. The restoration work was considerable, but he made it his own by collecting art and artifacts from all around the world, including Japanese wood blocks and a sunken bath that was able to accommodate six bathers with shoji doors. The gallery contained fine examples of pre-Columbian art, silk wall coverings, Chinese porcelain, Japanese fan paintings, Etruscan, Magna Grecia and Arrezzo ceramics. The European paintings, such as an original Monet titled 'Water Lily', graced the Red sitting room, as well as fine paintings in the Grey Room and a Napoleonic period bedroom. The drawing room and the master bedroom had mainly period French furniture of Louis XIV and XV, and were complimented by Greek and Egyptian artifacts. In the centre of the stable yard was a large cast iron figure of Punchinello, conspicuous by its white appearance contrasted by vivid red clown facial colors. A story was told of a hurling game in the ballroom of the house when the master was away. Not appreciating the value of the two vases that were used to make temporary goal posts, in a diving save by the goalkeeper the ball was stopped at the expense of knocking over one of the vases. Maybe the story has been embellished with age, but if true it was a costly save in the course of the game!

As Huston got his house and stables established he moved in with his wife Ricki and daughter Angelica and son Tony. The children who are now successful in the film industry, attended the Mercy Sisters School in nearby Loughrea, often spending time after school waiting for the chauffeur with Mrs. Tierney who was the mother of Martin who worked at St. Clerans. The children had a considerable amount of freedom riding their Connemara ponies, and Tony in particular was a fine fisherman at a young age. In fact Tierney who taught him how to cast a fly was particularly proud of his young student, and afterwards when he emigrated to America he would recount the prowess of young Tony Huston and his fly casting skills for fellow enthusiasts of the sport. As Huston divided his time and film commitments at home and abroad, there followed a succession of film stars visiting East Galway. Prior to that the locals had only seen film stars like John Wayne and Maureen O'Hara in the making of the film The Quiet Man. But some natives remember seeing the Mexican film star Movita visiting Loughrea with boxer Jack Doyle known as the 'Gorgeous Gael', and apparently Lil Duffy a local businesswoman is reputed to have whistled a song for the visit of the Prince of Wales to the town earlier in the century! With Huston's arrival that all changed, with screen and stage writers such as Arthur Miller and John-Paul Sartre working on film scores at St. Clerans, while others just came to visit like Montgomery Clift before shooting the film *Freud*. Gregory Peck who later owned the 1963 Leopardstown Chase winner Owen's Sedge trained by Tom Dreaper stayed at St. Clerans, as did Deborah Kerr who was very popular for her pleasant and engaging manner with the local people. Novelist John Steinbeck and his wife Elaine usually spent Christmas at St. Clerans, and is remembered for playing Santa Claus on Christmas morning to all the children whose parents were working on the estate. On one St. Stephen's Day (Boxing Day) during an impromptu Ceili Dance in Raftery's Pub in Craughwell after the hunt, Steinbeck looked after children while their parents danced away. A quite and unassuming man, and although a best selling author with many of his books made into films, he was not recognised locally, and could wander about without any difficulty. Other familiar faces were Ursula Andress, Jean Paul Belmondo, Audrey Hepburn and Burl Ives.

Hunting

In 1960 John Huston was invited to become joint master of the Galway Blazers Foxhounds, which was to last for a thoroughly enjoyable 10 seasons, combining a busy filming career together with being a master of foxhounds and that of a country squire. By this time he had become friends with other hunting enthusiasts such as Lord Peter Patrick and Lady Anne Hemphill of Tulira Castle, Pat and Derek de la Poer Trench of Woodlawn House and the author Anita Leslie who was related to Sir Winston Churchill and her husband Bill King, who was a decorated submarine commander in the Second World War, and who when over 60 years of age sailed around the world single handed in his yacht the 'Galway Blazer'. Other friends were Maria and Brigadier Edmond Mahony and Bea and Dick Lovett a former cavalry officer riding instructor. Paddy Pickersgill who was the huntsman of the Galway Blazers at the time was a boxing fan. As Huston had won a Golden Gloves title in America they followed and discussed their shared interest frequently. A lady called to the hunt kennels one evening intent on telling Pickersgill exactly what she thought of him. Considering it the greatest insult that she could think of, she told Pickersgill that he looked exactly like his dog. Meeting Huston the following day Pickersgill told him that he had been paid a great compliment by a lady the previous evening. Huston understood the twist in the story as he knew Pickersgill adored his dog Tiger, and looked on him as his best friend!

Lord Hemphill recalls when an attractive blue-eyed gentleman who was a house guest of Hustons wanted to buy a Connemara pony, and arrived over to Tulira Castle to look at the ponies in Lady Hemphill's Stud. He appeared satisfied with his selection, and as he walked back to his car Lady Hemphill remarked, "Sorry I did not catch your name". The visitor replied, "My name is Paul Newman "! As the friendship with the Hemphills developed Huston enjoyed joining Lord Hemphill on his yacht with his house guests sailing around the islands in Galway Bay. Another favorite stop for Huston and his guests was Paddy Burke's Pub in Clarenbridge well known for its Galway Bay oysters, where they had some good sing songs.

His stud groom Paddy Lynch describes Huston as 'A gentleman of gentlemen', with a deep interest and kindness for all his staff, and particularly their families. He was amazed that when he may have been away from home filming for months on end, and not having ridden a horse in the meantime, that on returning he would announce that he was going hunting the following day. He had no sense of danger and was very brave across country. Occasionally if he felt like making it a short day he was quite generous in handing his horse over as a spare ride to a delighted hunt follower. But Lynch made sure that his boss was well mounted, and acquired some of the best hunters for him. A few that came to mind were a very reliable horse named Smasher, and a horse called Saffron that he bought from P.P. Hogan the Scarteen Foxhounds field master. Hogan had a reputation as a fine judge of a horse, and is credited as the person who recommended Derby winner Nijinsky to owner Robert Sangster and trainer Vincent O'Brien. In fact Lynch has a photo on his sitting room wall of Huston and film actor Montgomery Clift with Smasher. But Huston had particular affection for three of his hunters, Naso, Daisy Belle and Frisco. I can recall as a teenager being in the right place at the right time when Huston had decided to have a short day hunting after returning from a long spell away filming. He was kind enough to offer his horse to me to hack him home, or continue in the hunt, but obviously I choose the latter. But I had to make one important adjustment, which was to wrap the stirrup leathers around the stirrups a couple of times to cater for my short legs, so sitting comfortably in his saddle I was away on his horse with the wind in my face across the Galway stone walls that I got to know so well. His wife Ricki although a novice rider was determined to hunt at least once, and through perseverance and expert tuition from Captain Ian Hume Dudgeon she did achieve her ambition.

Huston was not adverse to taking part on cross country runs, and one that stands out was a reenactment of the first steeple to steeple chase which was a run of five miles cross country over natural obstacles from Buttevant to Doneraile in County Cork, which P.P. Hogan won.

Horse Breeding

Huston got interested in horse breeding and particularly had in mind a Connemara Pony Stud, and would look forward to going on buying trips to Clifden Show with Ricki, Paddy Lynch and Betty O'Kelly. It started with the purchase of foundation mare Glen Nelly described as an oil painting, because of her near perfect conformation, and Killroe Star.

Young horses were occasionally bought in for producing as show hunters, and resulted in winning rosettes in the Middleweight and Heavyweight show classes at the RDS Horse Show.

Aside from Connemaras ponies, thoroughbred and show horses, the family were fortunate to produce a top class showjumper as well. Paddy Lynch got a call from one of the nuns in Kylemore Abbey Convent informing him that her brother's young horse was persistently jumping into the convent grounds, and would the Hustons like to buy him. Ricki Huston decided to buy him, and when Paddy hunted him a few times he discovered that he had an athletic jump in him. Known as Errigal he entered him for Ballinasloe Show and won three competitions on him in one day, taking two more the following year. He was by the same stallion Little Heaven, as the great Dundrum that represented Ireland ridden by Tommy Wade so many times all over Europe. To allow him to achieve his potential the horse was sold to Frank McGarry whose rider Francie Kearins took him to another level. The horse was later sold on and ridden internationally by Diana Connolly-Carew.

Leaving County Galway

After 18 years as owner and country squire of St. Clerans, and joint master of the Galway Blazers for ten seasons, with Brian Fanshawe, Jack Mahony, Frank Mannheim and Lord Peter Patrick Hemphill, John Huston reluctantly sold the estate and its contents. At that stage he was an Irish citizen, and he was sad to let what had become part of him go. He is remembered fondly in County Galway for his support of the Galway Blazers at an important time, and his kindness and generosity to his staff and his former neighbours. He was large in stature and even larger in life. Fortunately the corridors of St. Clerans still ring out with the lively conversations of guests, as it is now one of the best known Irish Manor Houses run on a commercial basis under the ownership of American television personality Merv Grifffin.

Paul Kinane, Gavin Duffy and Michael Kinane at Punchestown Races

Nancy Penn Smith Hannum

Nancy Penn Smith Hannum was born into a wealthy New York banking family. Her grandfather E.H. Harriman was master of the Orange County Hounds, then hunting an area north of New York. As the city developed he relocated his pack to the Plains of Virginia.

After the death of her father, her mother later married Mr. Plunkett Stewart who founded Mr. Stewart's Cheshire Hounds in Unionville, Pennsylvania. He quickly set about acquiring farms in the hunting country, removing wire fences and replacing them with post and rails which has made it to this day some of the finest and most open hunting country in the world. He added easements in the deeds of the properties to restrict development and protect the environment.

Nancy Penn Smith Hannum continued the practice of her stepfather while she was master and huntsman of the pack for over 50 seasons. She was a renowned hound breeder using many of the breeding lines from packs in England such as the Duke of Beaufort Foxhounds.

The classic painting in Nancy Penn Smith Hannum's drawing room by the celebrated American artist George Ford Morris, gives an insight into her family background, and their association with horses. It is a striking study of her riding her pony Sylvan Artist when she was 4 years of age, being led by her sister Carol who passed away in 1928. Both are impeccably dressed in matching costumes. Ford Morris was rated on the same level as an artist as Sir Alfred J. Munnings and Franklin Brooke Voss, considered as one of the three great animal portrait artists of his time. Morris who studied in Paris at the Academe Julien was never a gallery or exhibition artist, but painted mainly commissions, and had a studio opposite the old Waldorf Astoria Hotel on 33rd Street in Manhattan. His personal interests were in American Saddlebreds and Scottish Collies, and even the advertising posters that he painted for shows such as The National Horse Show in New York, and Dog Shows are much valued collectors items.

Nancy Penn Smith Hannum has had a remarkable life in hunting, hound breeding, horse breeding, racing, and the conservation of lands for habitat and foxhunting. She is known all over the hunting world respectfully as Mrs. Hannum, the legendary former master and huntsman of Mr. Stewart's Cheshire Hounds for over 50 seasons in Unionville, Pennsylvania.

Family life in New York
Her grandfather E.H. Harriman was a successful banker who lived on Long Island, and kept a pack of foxhounds, the Orange County Hounds kennelled on Arden Farms which is still in the family, and located near the American Army Military College at Westpoint, off Route 7 north of New York. Concerned about the sprawling city that was spoiling his hunting country, Harriman moved his horses, hounds and staff to the Plains of Virginia where they still hunt to this day. Her father R. Penn Smith who was also a joint master of the Orange County Hounds was also a banker, and managed Cassatt & Company later known as Merryl Lynch, Fenner & Bean in New York. Mr.Plunkett Stewart who was to become her stepfather, was manager of the bank's office in Philadelphia. Having already lost her sister as a child, there was another tragedy when her parents were planning an exciting hunting trip to England in 1929. The travelling party included her mother and father, as well as Mr. and Mrs Dick Mellon and Mr. Plunkett Stewart who all had planned to spend the Winter hunting with the Quorn, Belvoir and the Cottesmore Foxhounds in the Shires in England. But shortly before the party left for England her father died. Later it was decided by the families that as everything was already planned and paid for, that they should go ahead and ship their horses, grooms, house staff and luggage to England, and settle into their rented hunting box near to Melton Mowbray.

Home in Pennsylvania and Mr. Stewart's Cheshire Hounds
The following season after they returned home from hunting in England Mr. Stewart and her mother got married, and moved from Long Island to Unionville, Pennsylvania where they took over a pack of hounds which consisted mainly of American July and Walker hounds, and changed the name of the hunt to Mr. Stewart's Cheshire Hounds. Mrs. Hannum, although she was very young at the time, thought that the American hounds were the

best breed in the world, and now to her surprise Mr. Stewart was to change the pack over to English hounds drafted in from the Warwickshire, Cottesmore, Belvoir, Middlesex and the Fernie. Although Mrs Hannum originally disliked the English hound, she later changed her opinion having had some experience of working with them, and became a staunch supporter of English hounds all through her hunting career. She found them bidable, and adaptable, and her kennels saw a succession of visiting masters and huntsmen curious to see at first hand the results of her hound breeding policy.

Mr. Stewart's hunt country became unique in hunting, and because of Mr. Stewart's work with the farming community, the hunt country is one of the most open, crossable, and yet challenging of any hunting area in America. It started with Mr Stewart encouraging farmers to sell their land to him, and after he made the purchase he had what are termed easements, or clauses written into the deeds that restricted building development, and gave 'perpetual and exclusive foxhunting rights' thereby opening large tracts of land up to foxhunting. The arrangement was attractive to farmers as they were allowed to farm the land for the duration of their lifetime. After a farmer passed away, the 'lifetime rights' would then revert to Mr. Stewart. It was an offer that farmers could not refuse. Having done the deal Mr. Stewart removed any wire fences, and replaced them with posts, rails and panels designed to facilitate hunt followers to get through the country more easily. Today the Cheshire Hunt Conservancy continues to manage the hunt, and the hunting country, and the policy is continued by the present hunt committee. The hunt members are encouraged to buy any farms that come up for sale. But the strategy is not all to do with unlimited foxhunting rights, it also includes policies and practices on restricting housing development, and taking care of the environment, in terms of woodlands, flora, fauna and clean water, that has today shaped 30 square miles of some of the best hunting country in the world, and makes it an idyllic place to live in. Two of the largest farms that have come up for sale in recent years, that of Lammont du Pont's 5,200 acres and the Klebergs King Ranch which consisted of 6,500 acres for fattening the red Santa Gertrudis cattle shipped from Texas, before selling on in the New York cattle markets were successfully negotiated on behalf of hunting and the environment. But farm purchases were not confined to members of the hunt, as farmers were also invited to join the Conservancy in pass on deals for sections of the land. The Laurels, a tract of 800 acres was also negotiated, and now supplies most of the fresh water for the nearby town of Wilmington. Mrs. Hannum continued the tradition that her stepfather started. She also acknowledges the assistance of Frolic Weymouth, who founded the Brandywine Conservancy and is given a considerable amount of credit for negotiating the large landholding deals on behalf of hunting in the area. She smiled when I asked her had she any regrets, and still totally focused on foxhunting, said, that her only regret was that they did not buy the roads as well! When asked why Mr. Stewart and then Mrs. Hannum and other members of the Cheshire Hunt put in such an enormous amount of work, and their own personal money to shape the hunt country, the only reason she offered was because they 'Cared'. And because they 'Cared' the Cheshire hunting area is even conspicuous from the air, and known as the 'Black Hole'. From an aircraft if you look down at night as you approach Philadelphia Airport the whole area is light up with the exception of one black area. That is the Cheshire hunt area, and because of the lower density of housing it appears dark because of fewer lights! Because the Conservancy is so well established and respected by the Local Authorities, the policy of restricted development continues, providing those dwellings in the area with a local clean fresh water supply, and a natural habitat for flora and fauna, and of course unrestricted foxhunting.

Early School Days
Being from a wealthy family Mrs. Hannum's early school days in Unionville Public School had its setbacks, as she disliked being set apart from the other pupils by having the chauffeur drive her to school with her nanny. She felt that she was too conspicuous, and was delighted to change schools to Tower Hill in Wilmington, and then to Fox Croft boarding school in Virginia. She was joined at Fox Croft by her cousin Kathleen Harriman and friend Phylis Tuckerman, and they were delighted that they could even board their own horses at the school stables. This allowed her to hunt her horse Master Tom on the weekends with her grandfather's Orange County Hounds, hunted at the time by Duke Leach who used to use a cow horn hunting hounds. She also had the Piedmont and the Middleburg Hounds on her doorstep for variety. The head mistress Miss Charlotte Nolan was very supportive of the girls interest in hunting, especially when they decided to form their own beagle pack, the Fox Croft Beagles, with Mrs. Hannum as huntsman. Being continuously late for meals and classes in the first week of the pack being kennelled at the school, they decided to hire a kennel huntsman Buddy Downes, who was later to go on as whipper in of the Warrington Hounds. But Mrs. Hannum was no novice huntsman, as at home with the Cheshire Hounds she had spent her childhood tailing hounds, and rode up with the pack from the time she was 10 year of age, and was in full hunt livery whipping in when she was 15 years of age. Finished with school and back home hunting with the Cheshire Hounds, it became apparent that the huntsman Charlie Smith who was later elected to the Huntsman's Hall of Fame at Morgan Park Virginia was slowing down, and finding it difficult to

stay with his hounds. Mrs Hannum asked him if he would prefer to be relieved of the pressure as huntsman and he immediately agreed, so she took on the pack as huntsman.

Master and Huntsman of Mr. Stewart's Cheshire Hounds

Settled in Pennsylvania, she married John Hannum who became a Federal Court judge, and he shared her interests in the countryside. He was a familiar sight hunting. and an accomplished race rider, coming second twice in the Maryland Cup, and winning the Middleburg Cup and the Cheshire Bowl.

As a huntsman Mrs. Hannum had a tremendous voice, and was superb on the hunting horn. She was particular about her hound breeding, studying hound stud books and visiting England and Ireland for suitable outcrosses, and to this day she can recall accurately lines and pedigrees back for generations at will. She was a close friend of the 10th Duke of Beaufort who advised her on hound breeding policy, and many of her good stallion hounds were imported from his kennels at Badminton. Hounds were also acquired from the Oakley and the Cattistock. Although very definite about her preference in the fine points and characteristics of a well built hound, she would also consult with hunt staff and take their opinions on board. A hound she maintains must be well balanced, with a floating shoulder so that they can get by their ribs, not slapsided and have a level back. They also should have good feet, and be well balanced. She keeps emphasising that the challenge is not just to breed an individual hound, but to breed a pack of hounds that will hunt together, draw a covert properly even if the scent is difficult, and will get a fox on his legs and running quickly. She maintains that hounds will adapt to any country and get used to the elements and hark forward to a hound that is speaking. She sees lead hounds as in the role of a quarterback, similar to an American football team, with the lead hound calling the play. She enjoyed observing her pack of hounds struggle to find the line of a fox in a big covert, keeping their noses to the ground, determined to work out the line. Hunting her pack the emphasis was on 'Team Play', which meant she judged all her hounds on how they worked together as a pack.

In 50 seasons as master and huntsman she has by her own admission broken probably every bone in her body, which she regards only as an occupational hazard, and worth every break and fracture just to live her chosen way of life. But she always healed quickly as she was always very fit. She says you can learn to deal with pain, which often spells disaster for some people, but is just a discomfort to her. Even when she was in plaster or bandaged up and under doctor's orders through injury, she dismissed them as a minor inconvenience, and insisted in continuing her routine working in the kennels, which often meant walking the hounds that had not been hunting that day when she returned home from hunting. Although she was known for providing a high standard of sport for the Cheshire followers, the meet that she most likes to remember is as a child riding one of her favorite ponies Pussy Willow. The meet was near the village of Doe Run, when the doghounds found a good strong fox in the first covert, and took a line for the village of Lenape in the Brandywine country. They swung back through the east end and crossed Route 162, back to Unionville. Later at a check her mother suggested that she go home as her pony looked tired, but she was not giving up at this stage. The fox twisted again back over Route 162 and hounds accounted for him after a hunt of $5^1/_2$ hours The only finishers were the huntsman Charlie Smith and his whipper in Tom, her step father, her mother and herself

Race Riding

Unfortunately for Mrs. Hannum, ladies were not allowed to ride in point to points in the early part of her riding career when she would have been at her strongest as a rider. Later when the National Steeplechase Association was formed, and the restriction was lifted she took full advantage of the new rules allowing ladies to participate, and was a familiar figure at many of the hunt point to points.

As a hound breeder she has been in demand as a judge at hound shows, because of her knowledge of the hound stud book and her eye for conformation and movement. At the Cheshire hound shows she has invited many well known masters from other countries to judge at her shows including the Beaufort Foxhounds joint master and huntsman Captain Ian Farquhar.

Although retired as master of Mr. Stewart's Cheshire Hounds, and no longer riding, she nonetheless enjoys following hounds in her jeep. Unfortunately for her passengers she occasionally forgets that she is not on a horse, and in her enthusiasm continuously takes the well known shortcuts that she has learned from her years hunting hounds. If her jeep could jump then I am sure nobody would get between her and the pack.

Mr. Stewart's Cheshire Hounds continue to be one of the premier packs in America under the mastership of Nina Strawbridge, Bruce Miller and Russell Jones. They have a strong membership of enthusiastic racing followers, like successful trainer and jockey Paddy Nielson, as well as Clipper and Beth La Motte, Kathleen Crompton, Stuart and Kathy Malone and Dr. Chris Lyons. Their huntsman is Irishman Ivan Dowling, who developed his passion for foxhunting with the Galway Blazers in Ireland. Mrs. Hannum's family especially her son Jock and his son Jeb, and her nephew Cuyler's wife Katie still keep up the family tradition as regular followers of Mr. Stewart's Cheshire Hounds.

Toni de la Bouillerie

Toni de la Bouillerie is a member of the Codd family from County Wexford, well known in horseracing and hunting circles. Her mother bred winning National Hunt horses, and her brother was a successful jockey and producer of young racing stock.

When she went to live in Belgium she formed her own pack of hounds that she hunted around Brussels and the Ardennes. She later married Dr. Olivier de la Bouillerie who had his family pack of hounds near Saumur in France, and they amalgamated both packs into the Rallye des Grands Loups kennelled at his home, the Chateau de Lathan.

It seemed like the hunting season had only finished, when the Autumn hunting was beginning again. It is a time for the young hounds to be out for the first time with the adult hounds, building up their experience of crossing country as a unit in preparation for the coming season. But for a change I was hunting in the Anjou Region of France, known as the 'Garden of France' and famous for its fresh water crayfish, fruit and vegetables, and of course their Sauvignon Blanc, Chardonnay and Chenin Blanc grapes that are harvested to produce the region's fine white wines.

The opportunity arose as a result of a chance meeting when I was reporting on the Bree Foxhounds in County Wexford the previous year, when it was recommended that I go to France for some typical French Autumn hunting at Noyant north of Saumur. I was familiar with French staghunting having hunted with the Rallye Fountainbleu when I lived in France some years ago, but this time I was going hare hunting. The area around Saumur is probably better known as the home of the Ecole Nationale d'Equitation of France, or the French Equitation School where the famous Cadre Noir are based. The original Cadre Noir was founded in 1815 by the then King of France, Louis the XVIII, which then consisted only of military staff to train cavalry riders and horses. The present school was founded in 1972 and consists of a custom-built facility set on 300 hectares on two different sites, that is jointly sponsored by three French Ministries, Sport, Agriculture and Defence. The site has 42 riding masters, 5 farriers, 500 stables, 6 indoor arenas, 15 outdoor arenas and 50 kilometres of roads, tracks and a cross country course, as well as a fully staffed veterinary and research building. Its mission now is to train mainly civilian riders. During the year about 25,000 students attend 40 different courses, but to qualify to attend a course you have to have achieved set standards. They have a public relations role also insofar as they are obliged to give public demonstrations at home and abroad with the French riding horses, the Selle Francais and the Anglo Arab, to ensure that they are clearly identifiable as the French riding horse by the public.

The Irish connection with French hunting was Toni de la Bouillerie, whose maiden name was Toni Codd, a member of the well known Wexford racing and hunting family. Her father Patrick was a former master and huntsman of the Killinick Harriers, and her mother Eileen bred a number of successful National Hunt horses, particularly Sunny Bay who was twice runner up in the Aintree Grand National. Her brother Frank was a successful amateur jockey, and probably is best known for winning the Whitbred Gold Cup for trainer Edward O'Grady on Drumlargan. He now produces young horses for the racetrack.

Toni worked with John Watson who was the World Three Day Eventing silver medallist, riding his own horse Cambridge Blue at Lexington Kentucky when runner up to Bruce Davidson riding Might Tango in the World Championships in 1978. Having gained additional experience in Watson's she moved abroad to Belgium where she lost little time in forming the Rallye le Grandes Champs, her own pack of harriers, and she hunted them regularly around Brussels and the Ardennes. Helping to keep the lineup Irish, she had Una O'Neill another Wexford emigrant whipping in to her. Una is now attached to the Rallye de la Foret de Chaux who hunt wild boar at Chevanceaux just north of Bordeaux. When Toni formed a friendship with Dr. Olivier de la Bouillerie, besides making the decision to get married, they also had to make a decision on what they would do about hunting, as he had his own pack of hounds in France, and she had her pack in Belgium. So a compromise was reached when they decided to amalgamate both packs into the Rallye des Grands Loups now kennelled at Olivier's home, the Chateau de Lathan at Breil. The Chateau is all that one would imagine of a typically French chateau, with its complex of additional period buildings that enhance the main chateau, together with an imposing stone stable yard and kennels. The gardens contain beautiful laid out walks. It also features a maze which if we are to believe the mythical tale is if one manages to work the puzzle out, it leads one to a boat that takes one out to the island on the lake which is referred to as the Island of Love, and one is rewarded with a meeting with the love of one's life. It seemed at a glance to be quite easy, but unfortunately I did not have time to try my luck maybe it was because the love of my life was already on holidays with me at the time! These grounds are not alone for the benefit of the many tourists that visit during the summer months, but also for the 70 couple of hounds that are walked out through the grounds each evening. There are over 400 registered packs of hunting hounds in France and the previous weekend Toni and Olivier hosted the 34th Festival of Hare Hunting packs in the Park around the chateau, sponsored by the Camus Family, who are the last independent family of distillers of French cognac. Each country in Europe was allowed to enter two packs of hounds each, and packs travelled from many countries such as Italy and Sweden.

You would imagine that all of Toni and Olivier's hounds are French bred, but I should not have been surprised when they pointed out three of their best imports were from Ireland. They included a doghound named Oldcastle from the Tipperarys, and his two sons Shannon and Shamrock. From the Island Foxhounds in Wexford they had New Look, and Tullycana from the Killinicks all looking well in their adopted country and responding to all the commands from the huntsman in French. Ironically these hounds seem to adapt better to the French language than humans! Some of their offspring are with another pack hunting wild boar, again adapting well to a different quarry.

They hunt hare from November to March and have a special licence to hunt fox, wild boar and pine martin which are classified as vermin outside the regular season. This means that they are hunting practically for twelve months of the year. In between hunting their own hounds they also get out weekly with the local stag hounds, the Champ Chevrier which are one of the oldest packs in France. Their hunting area is a large geographic area in their own region, but they also hunt by invitation from landowners around Paris, Bordeaux and as far south as the Pyrenees, so it is not unusual for hounds and horses to travel long distances and hunt a particular area for a few days at a time.

I joined them for Autumn hunting outside the village of Bauge. There was a great turnout from the local gun club when we got to the meet. My horse was a Selle Francais which together with the Anglo Arab are the most common horses hunted. Olivier drew the ditches around large tracts of maize and sunflower fields and hounds quickly found a fox. He ran straight initially then turned righthanded and jinked left around the Chateau de Lamery but was accounted for as he crossed the road near Chavayne. The next draw produced another pilot who kept hounds on their toes as he ran through field after field of maize before they eventually lost him as the sun was rising, and the morning got warmer. Hounds were kept busy as we continued to jump numerous narrow ditches to stay in touch with them before Olivier blew for home.

The apre hunt refreshments were hosted by the local gun club at their clubhouse, aptly named the Société la Renaissance in the nearby village, which they share with the Boule Club. There was a choice of local rose wine for those that were taking it easy for the afternoon, and Orangina for those who had to go to work. It was a great experience to see this beautiful French countryside on horseback, following an experienced pack of carefully bred hounds, and above all an opportunity to enjoy typical French hospitality, and of course an Irish flavour provided by our host Toni de la Bouillerie to top it all off.

The Brosna Foxhounds

Alison Baker

Alison Baker and her family have been horse breeders for as long as they can remember. But in 1957 a very special foal was born as a result of the mating of their mare Bright Cherry and the stallion Archive. The foal bred by her mother Kathleen went on to be named Arkle who raced 35 times, winning 27 races and placed 7 times, and remarkably only on one occasion was he not in the first three finishers. He raced in the colours of the Dutchess of Westminister and was trained by Tom Dreaper, winning three Cheltenham Gold Cups, and is still considered as the greatest steeplechaser of all time.

His early education was done by Alison who affectionately named him Fellow. Aside from her interest in racehorses Alison was joint master of the Fingal Harriers Hunt, and enjoyed following hounds, jumping the wide ditches in north County Dublin and south County Meath.

The area around the village of the Naul in North County Dublin may not be considered the thoroughbred breeding center of Ireland, but when one looks a little closer, some real champions have been bred there by a small number of families. The late Richard (Dickie) Ball whose studfarms at Mooreside and Reynoldstown produced the famous Derby winner Ballymoss. He also bred Barbur winner of two Lincolns, and Star Kingdom who was the champion 3 year old in the Southern Hemisphere in the 1940's. In National Hunt racing he bred Reynoldstown, who won the Aintree Grand National on two occasions, his first was 75 years ago this year. The Maxwells stood his sire My Prince at their Man O War Stud not too far away.

Another family rose to prominence in the area, the Bakers, as they bred the great and arguably the greatest steeplechaser of all time, the mighty Arkle. The Bakers were substantial landowners at the Naul and also at Swords, following equine pursuits like hunting, point to pointing, and particularly breeding.

Their most successful broodmare was Bright Cherry, who was the dam of Arkle and whose current broodmares are all related.

Early days
Sisters Alison and June Baker reflected on their happy life in Malahow, and some of their earliest memories and their families association with horses. Their father T.K.H. (Harry) Baker was a large cattle and sheep farmer, who also bred thoroughbred horses. Their mother Mary Kathleen Christie hailed from Newtown House in Swords. As children they shared an interest in ponies with their sisters Do Do, Pidgie and brother Harry. They all hunted with the Fingal Harriers and the Ward Union Staghounds. Alison later became joint master of the Fingals with Jimmy Ryan and John Purfield. When the Fingal Harriers were invited some years ago to parade their hounds in the main arena of the Royal Dublin Society their affable huntsman of 40 seasons the late Paddy Shanahan spent the early part of the Summer preparing his hounds for the prestigious occasion. At that time there was a double and single bank in the main arena of the showgrounds in Ballsbridge. Alison as a joint master was part of the Fingal group of masters parading. The crowd encouraged them to jump the banks, and Alison duly obliged, and even jumped them a second time when the spectators called for an encore.

Her sister Pidgie was a familiar sight in the hunting field riding one of her favorite horses Mister Hudson, who was aptly named, as he was a real gentleman and measured each ditch with precision.

The Bakers were associated with many good horses like Bomber Command, and Kai Lung both winners in Baldoyle and the Phoenix Park. On Alisons 21st birthday her father gave her a present of My Richard, out of Greenogue Princess, who won the Fingal Harriers Hunt Cup at Mooreside, ridden by PP Hogan.

Bright Cherry
Arkle's dam Bright Cherry by Knight of the Garter out of Greenogue Princess by My Prince, had an impressive racing record in her own right. She won the Easter Chase at Fairyhouse and five other chases, as well as one hurdle race, and was placed eleven times. Her jockeys were Pat Taaffe, TP Burns and Eddie Newman, She was a fast mare, and passed it on to her progeny such as

Cherry Tang in 1952, Cherry Bud 1955, Saval Beg 1963, Golden Sparkle 1964, Cherry Wine 1966, and of course her star son Arkle foaled in 1957, by Archive who stood at Loughtown Stud, then owned by the Vard family. A number of Bright Cherry's progeny went on to breed winners such as Cherry Bud, the dam of Vulture who won a bumper at Fairyhouse when ridden by Barry Brogan. He was to win again under James English who changed careers shortly afterwards, and is now a successful artist, and was recently honoured by being elected a member of the Royal Hibernian Academy. During his ride on Vulture English's mother is reputed to have prayed in the local church that her son would win, and her prayers were answered! But Vulture nearly achieved his finest hour when he was narrowly beaten into second place in the Aintree Grand National. His full brother Colebridge was a multiple winner, which included an Irish Grand National, and third in the Cheltenham Gold Cup, and was later sold to General Mellon in America. Golden Sparkle won for their neighbour Pat Rooney. Breeding racehorses is not all rosy, it is often a game of patience, trying to make the right decisions, and not losing faith at setbacks and disappointments. The Bakers have no doubt had some outstanding successes, but also disappointments when you consider the breeding record of their good mare Bright Cherry. It runs as follows, bred six live foals, slipped two and was barren eleven times.

Bright Cherry was buried in the Quarry Field in Malahow on the 25th June 1971, where she reared her famous son, and the site is marked by a specially commissioned granite headstone, which will mark for posterity the final resting place of this very special mare.

Arkle

The decision to send Bright Cherry to Archive, Arkle's sire, came about as a result of a family discussion. Her father often talked about Archive and felt that at some stage he would like to use him on one of their mares. He liked the fact that Archive who was by Nearco and had speed also on his dam side through Book Law, might pass it on through her son. Alison and June remember Bright Cherry going to be foaled in Ballymacoll Stud in Dunboyne, as she was to be covered by Dorothy Pagets horse Straight Deal that was standing there. The gangly foal that was to become the greatest steeplechaser, Arkle, was not a big foal and not very angular. He was delivered by the stud on a very stormy day to the family farm at Malahow. Alison recognised that he was different as she felt that he had brains, as he was always the first to come over to be fed. He was also very curious as a foal, and loved people, and she called him 'Fellow'. She did the early breaking work on him, having handled him well over his early years, so that he was ready for backing when he was sold on. He was prepared for the sales, and was one of two horses bought by the Duchess of Westminister and shipped to England. Tom Dreaper was asked to go over and take his pick, and he chose Arkle as he had broken and ridden his dam Bright Cherry. He stood 16.1 hands with high withers but was not a robust horse. In his first race, the Lough Ennel Maiden Plate a bumper in Mullingar he was third ridden by Mark Hely Hutchinson. His first win was on a very wet day in Navan in a three mile hurdle in bottomless conditions, when he had to take on the hot favourite Kerfro ridden by Pat Taaffe. Liam McLoughlin was on board and Arkle came home in style, beating Kerfro. Because of the bad weather the Bakers decided not to travel, but their neighbour Johnny Sherwin called that evening with the good news that Arkle had won the Bective Hurdle. The Bakers then travelled to Leopardstown where Height of Fashion gave him a good run, with Arkle carrying 12 stone 7 pounds.

For his first Cheltenham Gold Cup Alison, June and their brother Harry went over for the race. The weather conditions were bad with constant snow showers. Despite the weather they had a picnic in the car park. Alison got the wish bone of the chicken, and of course her wish was that Arkle would win, and he duly obliged against the mighty English challenger Mill House ridden by Willie Robinson. The crowd were ecstatic, Arkle looked around as he was always the crowd pleaser. The Bakers got over the rails but could not get down off the stand to the winners enclosure, as the crowds streamed down to greet the winner. He was to go on and win another two Cheltenham Gold Cups in1965 and 1966.

Arkle not alone created history in the Gold Cup, but his racing record reads, raced 35 times, won 27, 2nd twice, 3rd three times, 4th twice and unplaced once, giving lumps of weight away in nearly all his races. He was very much a celebrity with lots of fan mail arriving to his stable at Dreapers, as well as being invited to parade at various events. On one occasion he was paraded at the RDS ridden by Pat Taaffe, and the crowd were asked to be quiet in case they would startle him. At first he paraded at a lackluster pace, but the crowd could not contain themselves and burst into cheering and applause. Arkle immediately was on his toes and really strutted his stuff. The end of his career came when he injured his pedal bone in the King George Chase VI at Kempton, but despite carrying the injury and top weight he was still runner up to Dormant. He was laid up for some time, and nearly made a comeback at Fairyhouse, but it was decided not to run him on the frosty ground. Eventually he got arthritis so it was decided to put him down humanely. He was buried in Bryanstown Stud then owned by the Dutchess of Westminister, and later his remains were moved to The Irish National Stud.

Alison feels Arkle was a lucky horse, as he had the advantage of being well minded from the time he was a foal, as well as having a sympathetic owner in the Duchess of Westminister, a patient trainer in Tom Dreaper and a top class jockey in Pat Taaffe.

To Alison and June Baker Arkle was special even as a foal. Today they still live on the family farm at Malahow near the Naul. They still have their brood mares all related to Arkle and the Bright Cherry line. The current young stock are by Alderbrook and Arctic Lord. They regularly travel to their favorite race meetings, and also visit their trainer Jim Dreaper, to see their horse Cherry Hunter by Treasure Hunter out of Clever Cherry who has already won on the flat, over hurdles and chasing, the most recent win in Punchestown, when ridden by Jim's son Thomas.

The family tradition in hunting and horses lives on in the Baker family, as Alison and June's nephew David rarely misses a week hunting with the Ward Union Staghounds and the Fingal Harriers, and his brother John is a staunch supporter as well.

In the course of our discussion it became apparent that there is no significant monument in memory of Arkle on any racecourse in Ireland, as there is for example to Red Rum in Aintree, and Dawn Run at Cheltenham. It would indeed be a nice gesture to install something similar in Ireland, and would be a fitting monument to honor Bright Cherry, Arkle and the Baker family. For a small village like the Naul in north County Dublin it certainly has produced some very special horses.

Susanne Macken, Brian Munn and Lt. Col. Dennis Foster at Punchestown Races

Francie Derwin

Francie Derwin was known in his time as the largest horse dealer in Ireland, and was a familiar figure at many of the horse fairs around the country.

He was a self made man, as his parents passed away when he was 12 years old. Despite the fact that he started off with little capital, he opened up a large trade in horses and ponies in Continental Europe and America.

Most of his family continued the tradition, and went on and competed for Ireland in showjumping, as well as training point to pointers for the racing season.

The Derwin family are probably one of the best known families associated with horse dealing in Ireland, and the man that started it all, Francie Derwin was one of those fascinating people, who from humble beginnings, became one of the largest horse dealers in Ireland. He bought and sold literally thousands of horses and ponies to all parts of the world. He passed away at the young age of 59 years, but he has left a legacy through the knowledge he managed to impart to the family that the Derwins are still the people you have to bid against at the sales and fairs if you want to buy that special horse or pony. It is strange that for Francie money was not the main motivation. It was said that if you gave him a million Euros it would make no difference to him. And although profit was important, it was much more about the kick he got from doing a good deal. It was a social thing too, as his customers were his friends. The yardstick was on how good his judgment was in what he paid for horses when he bought them, and how well he could sell them. It is the adrenaline, the buzz that he got that kept him going. But resilience and self belief are often the hallmarks of successful businessmen.

The early days

Derwin had a natural gift for judging a horse, at a glance. He never used a vet to check if a horse was sound, regardless of how much he paid for them, and he had to pay enough for the good ones. It was always down to his instinctive judgment if a horse was sound. But he would also have a good look at the seller because that could tell him a lot too.

Francie Derwin was born in Creggan outside Athlone. His parents passed away when he was very young, so at 12 years of age he went to a horse fair in Athenry and bought a horse and rode it home to Athlone, a distance of perhaps 40 miles. When he sold that horse it was the beginning of Francie taking his early steps to becoming a legendary horse dealer. He continued to buy and sell locally until he built up the numbers. In the early days on a Sunday night he would set off on the road with perhaps up to 20 horses, with him tucked up in a pony and trap to be on time for the fair in Longford on Monday morning. Some of his customers at that time were Frank Kiernan from Crossmaglen, Timmy Horgan from Cork, the Coopers from Dublin who used to buy a lot of horses for CIE the national transport company, and also sent horses to Hollwells in England. Marshall Parkhill bought black horses all about 16 hands for the Troopers. As the numbers of horses being traded increased Francie had to hire cattle trucks so that he could get to fairs like Tallowroe, Cahirmee and Ballinasloe. His main market at this stage was to dealers, so horses and ponies were sold on the halter, as long as they were 'the right model'. Other customers in England were Jim Gambell and Bob Jolly who used to ride for Gambell. Michael Enright in Askeaton would find the nice horses in the Limerick area. As many as 20 horses and ponies were being shipped out each week in the '60s and '70s. To demonstrate how good a salesman Francie was, his wife Ann tells the story of one morning a couple who were going off on holidays to Spain arrived in his yard with a horse that they wanted Francie to buy. The couple left some time later with three horses as Francie instead of buying theirs, sold them two more instead! When farmers had a horse to sell they would simply phone Francie.

He met his wife Ann one day when he loaned her a cob to go hunting. They shared a common interest in horses and they married and reared a family of four children, Pamela, Tanya, Jim and Francis.

Hunting, Racing and Showjumping

All the children turned out to be accomplished riders. Every week the truck was loaded up and the children went everywhere with them, whether it was to fairs, sales, shows, racing or hunting, it was like a permanent holiday. They all hunted and raced during the winter and showjumped in the summer. During that time Ann was master of the Westmeath Harriers. She also took out a trainer's licence in 1971 and had success with horses like Bucksbridge and Nickis Joy with many of the top jockeys of that era riding for her like Tony Martin, Dessie Hughes Anthony Powell and Frank Berry. All the time they were developing their dealing business as well. As the children got older they were mounted on better ponies, and they all went on to compete at all the shows around Ireland, winning regularly in the RDS in Dublin and all around Europe. They also went on to earn International honours as well. One of their best ponies was Dusty Boy bought from Quinns in Ennis, who won numerous major competitions, and later represented England at International level. Quite a number of the top jumping ponies in America, Switzerland, France and Sweden were produced by the family, like Kiltormer and Ballybin. Robert Smith's top horse Brookstreet Clover was a Derwin horse. The boys also rode in point to points and Jim had a good horse Friers Island, that he rode to win a number of races including the Barber Cup in Castletown. He was sold on for Hunt Chasing in England. Francie loved point to points, and owned a number of good horses like Tiger Bay and Carrigflame that he got very attached to. During this time the competition horses in the yard were ridden by David McCormack. With more exposure in showjumping the family continued to develop a reputation for producing top class showjumpers. The trade was 90% export while 10% was in Ireland. The family loved the land and own a number of farms in the county as well as Friers Island, a 180 acre island just outside Athlone on the Shannon. They bought it when, as they say in the trade, 'they got a touch' on Nickis Joy in 1980, a horse that they sold on at a good price, which helped to part finance the purchase. There is a lane onto the island, so they built a crosscountry course that can be used all year around. It has to be remembered that bank interest rates around his time went up to 19%, so it was not all a roller coaster ride, as horses had to be sold to meet bank commitments. Often there could be 400 horses and ponies on the farm, and one would wonder how Francie Derwin would remember which was which. But he would always know if one was missing, and his way of remembering them was either by colouring, or he had the ability to identify a unique marking on all his horses. He would sell thousands of horses in a year, often up to 70 a week. It is impossible to track all the good horses that they sold over the years, as for many years no papers were available on the breeding, and horses were usually renamed when they left the country by their new owners

The Legacy - Passing on the tradition
Francie would always have somebody in mind for a horse, and he was always on duty even in hospital a few days before he passed away with the help of

his mobile phone. He had great courage and self confidence, and never cared what the breeding of an animal was as long as it was what he called a good model. His legacy was the skill, judgment and confidence that he imparted to his family, that still makes them the huge dealers that they are today. He never liked warmblood horses, he called them foreigners, and said he could always recognise them by their feet and their heads. He was adamant that people don't come to Ireland to buy warmblood horses. He maintained that a warmblood while they may be flashy, they never continue to improve like an Irish bred, and that they don't help the trade in Irish horses.

The tradition is carried on by Francie's wife Ann who runs her own yard from her farm at Ballymore near Athlone. She attends most of the main sales and buys suitable horses for clients, while keeping hunters and also breeding and racing point to pointers. Jim and Francis run separate businesses from the old yard in the middle of Athlone. Tanya and Pamela have taken a break from the horse business and work in Athlone. They are still the main dealers at the top fairs and sales. Jim and Francis would have 300 to 400 horses and ponies at any one time with up to 75 stabled and in work, and local riders do most of the competition work. They don't break horses any more, as they usually buy them as 4 year olds and upwards already broken. Jim rates Ballinasloe still as a great place to buy horses, even if the prices have gotten a little higher. At a recent fair he bought 40 horses in the course of a week. They have had some nice horses competing like Royal Cruise, Paddy Blue and Little Jake who was second in Millstreet. Jim has a couple of thoroughbred mares, one of which has progeny by Aldebrook, and a couple of point to pointers, Tupacanra by Supreme Leader that his Dad bought in Longford, and On The Drink. that his mother named. They have a concern with the hunting ban in the UK that it could affect trade, as a large number of horse being bred in Ireland today will never graduate to be showjumpers or eventers, so it is difficult to see where the replacement market would be at the moment.

All of the family are unanimous in saying that Francie was unique, he had that special gift with horses, and although he is greatly missed, he passed on many of his skills to his family.

He had a saying "One man planning is worth two men working". It worked for Francie Derwin.

Willie Leahy

Willie Leahy hunts as field master of the Galway Blazer Foxhounds during the Winter, and runs his Connemara Horse Trail business in the Summer, where he explores the wild bogs, seashores and mountains of Connemara with the increasing number of visitors that come on their annual vacation from many countries.

Having started his horse enterprise in the 1950's with one Irish Draught horse, he now owns the largest herd of Connemara ponies in the world, and exports the progeny to many parts of the globe. His Horse Museum at Dartfield in County Galway is dedicated to the Irish horse. He also keeps a number of seasoned hunting horses for visitors that come to hunt in Ireland.

In recognition of his business enterprise he was short listed for an award for Irish entrepreneurs which included visiting Harvard University in Boston. As always he is a practical person, and in his conclusions about the lecturers at Harvard he commented, "I could not do their job, and they certainly could not do mine".

Willie Leahy the well known horseman from Aille Cross outside Loughrea in County Galway reached the short list of 24 finalists in Ireland of the Ernst & Young Entrepreneur of the Year. Well, according to Willie he sees it as a recognition that the range of equestrian products that he has developed in the horse industry are now recognised as world class. He said it was great to sit alongside successful people from all parts of Ireland, who had one thing in common, that they all started with an idea and worked to make that idea a successful business. In the process they have all significantly contributed both economically and culturally to each of their own parts of Ireland. He has the height of praise for the sponsors, Ernst & Young, who recognised the diversity of each of the finalists in their own specific field. What pleased him in the final was that another horse enthusiast Dr. Peter Fitzgerald of Randox Laboratories won the top award. Beside the 'school of hard knocks' which is life, the last school that Willie attended was the local country school at Aille Cross in County Galway. So what was it like sitting in a lecture theatre in the hallowed halls of Harvard University outside Boston? He just feels that he learned a lot, and is stronger as a result of being there, mostly spending time with the other finalists. Although he was impressed with the various lecturers in Harvard, he is in no doubt as he remarked "I could not do their job and they certainly could not do mine"!

He is extremely proud of what he has achieved, not from a material point of view, but just that sense of achievement that drives self-made people. Today his business interests range from the Dartfield Horse Park and Museum, the Connemara Trail, the Aille Cross Winter Trail, hirelings to the Galway Blazers and adjacent packs, and the largest Connemara Pony breeding and sales operation in the world, as well as a supplier of hunters, show jumpers and eventers that are exported to all parts of the globe.

Getting started
It all started in the 1950's when he paid £10 for a horse which he trained and sold later at Loughrea Fair for £55, which was a tidy sum in those times. His philosophy was for every horse he sold, he would buy two more. That stock has increased to over 400 Connemara ponies and as many more horses. His second purchase was a chestnut Irish Draught horse named Dan, and a grey pony that he named Aille Castle. At a flapper race meeting in Eyrecourt County Galway the pony won not only the pony race but the horse race as well. Later in the afternoon he won the main showjumping competition. Mick Cash persuaded Willie's uncle to sell the pony for £250, but Willie felt that he was sold cheap, and he was so upset that his uncle felt sorry for him and gave him £50 to go and buy something else. He bought a very difficult horse for £37, and within a short time he got the better of the horse mainly by doing farm work with him like contract ploughing and spraying potatoes, and later sold him to Ned Cash for £135. Willie always liked to compete on his horses and although he says that he never managed to beat the mighty Dundrum and Tommy Wade, he did manage to divide the high pole competition with the great horse Ballingarry at Portumna Show. He also had a short but successful career

point to pointing having won the Blazers Members Race on Binhigh, a horse he bought from Patsy Corcoran, against a horse that was specially shipped over from England by Claude Fore to win it. Willie beat Claude's horse landing a 25/1 touch. Claude, keen to switch jockeys, asked Willie to ride his horse the following week and he won again. He also won the last race over a bank course that was run at the East Galway.

Hunter Hirelings

His next venture was to build up his hireling business, supplying horses to a number of different packs, the Blazers, Ormond, North Galways and the East Galways. He was quick to acknowledge the assistance that the Blazers master Michael Dempsey gave him while Michael was hunting the East Galways at the time. Very few people owned horse trailers in those early days so all the horses were hacked to the meets , some of which were over 20 miles away. It was not unusual to see Willie and his friends including the author hacking three horses each down the Lake Road in Loughrea on their way to meets at 8 o'clock in the morning, and later in the dark hacking back home after a day's hunting. To this day he not alone acts as field master to the Blazers who still hunt three day a week, but he also is one of the main suppliers of hirelings to the hunt.

Connemara Trail

The idea of the Connemara Trail came as a result of standing in the stable yard one day when he was wondering what to do with all his horses that were looking over their stable doors on a beautiful morning at the end of the hunting season. The idea came to him that maybe there were people out there that were not interested in hunting, but would be more interested in exploring the rugged and picturesque landscapes of Connemara on horseback. So never one to sit on an idea, that afternoon he went to the Tourist Office in Galway and asked them if they would keep him in mind if they got any inquiries. Within weeks they had a party of 26 French visitors booked for the Connemara Trail, but Willie did not have 26 horses, so his friends loaned him horses to get started. Today 35 years later the Connemara Trail which starts outside Galway and ends near Clifden is often fully booked in advance with visitors from all over the world, and such is its popularity that people return year after year. In fact one man has been back 27 times. After a day in the saddle exploring areas and scenery that are only assessable on horseback, customers stay in all the best hotels along the way experiencing the highest quality of food and hospitality. Foreign languages are not a problem as it is well known that Willie's charm translates easily to all languages.

Connemara pony breeding

As his hireling business and the Connemara pony business grew, so did his horse and pony sales. It was quite by accident that he got into such a large Connemara pony breeding operation, now recognised as the largest in the world with over 400 ponies. Some years ago he had a large order of Connemara ponies destined for a French customer cancelled. Willie feels he was fortunate, as what he considers the best Connemera stallion he is ever likely to own, Grangefinn Sparrow who is standing in America was part of the cancelled order. So he set about running him with the mares on his farms in Connemara and in Loughrea. Today if you visit the Horse Museum at Dartfield on the main Dublin road outside Loughrea you will see part of the herd of a couple of hundred Connemara mares and foals grazing around the Park. The rest of the herd roam and breed naturally in Connemara.

Dartfield Horse Museum

The Horse Museum at Dartfield on 350 acres was on his mind for many years, but because he was so busy it is only recently that he had the time to get the project finished. He felt that, although Ireland is known worldwide for the quality of Irish horses, Ireland lacked a quality horse museum. Today after an investment of over £4 million, visitors and particularly school children can take tours through a custom built museum of 20,000 square feet and learn the history of the horse from its evolution to the present day. It is made even more interesting by the use of various audio visual techniques. In addition, he has a rare collection of tack, carriages, stable equipment, riding clothes, photographs and paintings which approach the subject from various interesting dimensions. Outside in the park visitors can see part of the breeding operation, and walk the international three day event course with its variety of challenging obstacles. The centre also hosts corporate days with archery and clay pigeon shoots. A future project is the restoration of the old stone house in the park originally built by Robert Blake about 1815 to period standard.

Knowing the names of a lot of very famous people that he has sold horses and ponies to, he is very modest and makes no distinction between them, as he feels that every customer of his is special no matter what station in life they come from. But it is well know that Chelsea Clinton the daughter of former American President Bill Clinton was a visitor, and Mark Phillips the former husband of Princess Anne together with many more world figures that would be well known to the general public.

I was curious as to whether he ever sought advice from anybody as he developed his business, and he simply said no, as he found that you could be easily put off by people who only see the pitfalls of developing a business idea, and don't see the positive side of making a business dream a reality.

So what is Willie Leahy's philosophy on life? Well, it is made up of a number of thoughts, like, give to others what you would like to get yourself, be determined and work hard, keep improving what you are doing and strive to be the best. He wants to leave something positive behind for generations to come, and above all he feels strongly that we should be proud of the Irish horse, the land and ourselves. It certainly has worked for Willie Leahy.

Connemara Mare and Foal at Dartfield Horse Park

Thady Ryan

Thady Ryan was one of the best known master of foxhounds in the world, and hunted the family pack, the Scarteen 'Black and Tan' Hounds for most of his life before handing over to his son Chris. The pack has been owned by the Ryan family for over 400 years.

A lifelong breeder of the Irish horse, even when he retired to his wife Anne's home country of New Zealand, he brought out an Irish Draught stallion and two brood mares to start off a breeding enterprise at their new home.

He and Anne came up with the idea of the hunt chase which has been such a popular event in the Summer season, attracting a significant number of spectators at shows all around the country.

Thady Ryan was an author, and a former Chef d'Equipe to Irish Olympic eventing teams in Japan and Mexico.

Although the life of that great master of hounds Thady Ryan's is well chronicled in two interesting books, *The Ryan Family and the Scarteen Hounds* by Michael MacEwan, and more recently with Thady's own book, *My Privileged Life*, I had the opportunity to meet him following the meet at Knocklong Hill in 2004, before he returned to his other home in New Zealand. I put a few questions of my own to him that I was always curious about. He is such pleasant company that time passes very quickly when discussing hounds and hunting. Besides being one of the most admired huntsmen and breeder of hounds in the world of hunting, he also has those wonderful characteristics like passion for the sport of hunting, a gentleman in all respects whether talking about his close knit family, his admiration of the farming community, the outdoor way of life or his spirituality.

Few packs of hounds have created so much mystery about their origins than the Scarteen, also known as the Black and Tans because of their distinctive colour markings. Some say that they originated from hounds that swam ashore when the Spanish Armada ships sank off the west coast of Ireland about 1588.

Another and probably more credible explanation is that the soldiers in the Spanish Garrisons, which were also trading posts based in Dingle and Ventry in County Kerry many years ago used to hunt for a pastime particularly on Valentia Island. They did not consider the Irish wolfhound fast enough, and eventually brought their own hounds to the island, now known as the Kerry Beagle. Maybe there is some truth in all of those theories as since then there have been infusions of blood from the French Gascon-Ariegeois, and nowadays there are very close breeding ties with hounds from the Kerry Foot packs.

The pack has been in the Ryan family since 1640, and during that time because of family tradition a member of the Ryan family has always hunted the pack, with the exception of a period following the time of the economic downturn known as the Depression. They were taken on then by Dr. Cecil MacLoughlin and Major Sir Cecil Walker, with huntsmen like Thady's brother-in-law Claude Thompson, Joe Pickersgill, Captain George Barker and David Price hunting the pack. But hunting the Scarteen Hounds presented a challenge to all of them, particularly those that were used to hunting English hounds, as the Scarteens do not like to be handled with the same discipline. They work best when a huntsman adapts to them and gets to understand them, rather than they adapting to the huntsman.

Introduction to hunting.
His father John took him hunting at his first meet at Scarteen when he was 7 years old. From then on he hunted regularly as school terms allowed him, before he went to Ampleforth College where they had a pack of beagles. The Kennel Huntsman who served 30 seasons in the college was Jack Welch, who he credits together with his father as being the two people who most influenced his early life to be a huntsman. He took on the College pack and hunted them for a season, and got his first introduction to the Peterborough Hound Show, producing Ampleforth Ringwood to win the Championship. Later as a serving master he was invited back to judge the beagle class.

He became joint master of the Scarteens in 1946 hunting hounds for 40 seasons. Whipping in to Thady for all that time was Tommy O'Dwyer now over 50 seasons with the Scarteens starting work in the kennels in 1952 when he was 14 years of age. Thady regrettably made the decision to retire as huntsman when he developed a heart condition, which after surgery allowed him to continue hunting. However he handed over the horn in 1986 to his son Chris who was then 27 years of age and who had just set himself up as a racehorse trainer at Scarteen. He is unique amongst huntsmen as he is both a fine horseman having ridden winners between the flags, and a natural handler of a pack of hounds.

As usual there were some amusing incidents in the course of Thadys' hunting life. One day he recounted that hounds ran hard at the back of Scarteen crossing the railway line on the brush of their fox. Thady's father John had the key to the railway gates. Being a devout Catholic he had his rosary beads also in his pocket which were mixed up with the railway gate keys. Extracting the bundle from his pocket and not having time to separate them it appeared obviously incorrectly to an English visitor that he opened the gate with his rosary beads. On his return to England he informed all his friends of the mystical powers of the Master of the Scarteens John Ryan!

On another occasion when negotiating the Black Trench which is reputed to be the most imposing natural obstacle in the Scarteen hunt country, a visitor was asked to describe the experience. He said that the trench is so wide that a rider has the time to start and finish 'The Lord's Prayer' from take off to landing!

When hunting in England with Lord Vestey, he recalled that after hunting, a black tie dinner had been arranged for the American and Irish visitors at Vestey's palatial mansion. The American master of the Midland Hounds Maison Lampton arriving back somewhat later than the others met Vestey in the huge entrance hall of his mansion, that would dwarf most buildings, and looking around the vast hall remarked "Well Vestey, humble but adequate"!

Favorite Horse

He had many wonderful horses but the horse that stands out most was Jacko, bred in Millstreet and bought by Noel C Duggan as a 3 year old. He was then bought by James Breen at Tallow Fair in County Waterford. He phoned Thady one evening and he described the horse to him as, 'Just your handwriting'. Thady did not rate his own handwriting so he was not sure what to expect. The horse hunted until he was 28 years old and lived out a happy retirement until passing away at the ripe old age of 40 years.

The other horse he talks about with affection is The Villian, bought from International Three Day Eventer and Bloodstock breeder Alan Lillingston who he also evented. Competing one day in Punchestown when jumping the third fence on the cross-country section, the horse mistook the beginning of the sandy surface on front of the fence as a ground line, and took off too far out and had a crashing fall. One lady competing in the roads and tracks said it was the nearest thing to seeing a horse and rider killed, but they survived and concentrated on hunting from then on.

Of course Thady also produced probably the best event horse that ever represented Ireland, that is Durlas Eile, that Major Eddie Boylan won a World Championship on. Thady also has the distinction of being Chef d' Equipe to Irelands Olympic Games Three Day Event Teams in both Tokyo and Mexico.

Favorite Hound

Juggler was his favorite hound. He was a pure Kerry hound with no outcross in him. He described him as having guts. He had a great understanding with the hound. One day at Garrydulas, Juggler started to draw a piece of bog with the pack, but before he went into the furze he looked around at Thady as if to say 'There is a fox in it Master', will I go ahead? Thady nodded at his favourite hound who immediately as if on command dived into the covert and had the fox on the move in an instant.

The other hound he liked was Hyder who with Highlight he considered was the best injection of Kerry blood into the Scarteens in recent years.

Hunting Packs and Huntsmen

Without doubt he had the height of respect for the Kerry Footpacks. He credits the followers with being exceptional sportsmen, and extremely knowledgeable on hunting and hounds. He also admired Elsie and Tom Morgan's West Waterford Hounds who he has occasionally hunted with at arranged joint meets, and the white College Valley and Border Hounds in England.

As for huntsmen he admires he considers this a very easy question, as without hesitation it is his son Chris who he is extremely proud of, and who has now hunted the pack for the last 18 seasons, and his father John who preceeded him as huntsman.

The Future of Hunting

It is interesting that the Irish Tourist Board actively promoted foxhunting overseas some years ago with considerable success. They were supported by Thady and Anne Ryan amongst others, who travelled to various events around the world. Hunting visitors to Ireland were made welcome, and hotels and guest houses saw an increase in their business, and more farmers got into hirelings. When a visitor had an enjoyable hunt on a hireling they invariably wanted to buy the horse and take him home. It was a very good campaign, which was a great boost for the sport horse business.

He sees hunting as going on indefinitely, as country sports are so ingrained in Irish people and their way of life. He cannot understand the Blair Government in the UK when there are so many serious problems in the world, and the blatant injustices to people and their lives, that their government would waste so much precious Parliamentary time arguing about hunting and fail to see the positive side to it.

He feels strongly about hunt followers appreciating the absolute privilege of being allowed to cross farmer's lands. He stresses that they should at all times demonstrate their gratitude to landowners and be courteous and supportive to them. He is proud to describe the Scarteens as a farmer's pack, and it is this factor that makes it the popular hunt that it is today.

The Concept of the Hunt Chase

He was judging at Charleville Show when he met Van de Vater. He said that he had to think up a new event for the Royal Dublin Society Annual Show. Van responded by saying that whatever the idea was that it had to have some association with hunting. So he sat down with his wife Anne and they explored various ideas and eventually put the idea of the Hunt Chase to the Royal Dublin Society Show Committee. They were slightly skeptical and suggested that he go away and raise the sponsorship which he did with the Quinnsworth Supermarket chain coming in as main sponsor. So it has gone from strength to strength since then, with a feature chase event at most shows in Ireland including a number in Britain as well, the largest of which is held at the Royal Show at Stoneleigh.

Boards and Associations

Thady Ryan was an innovator, and always wanted to add value to any organisation that he was associated with, particularly if it benefited the Irish half-bred horse. He was a founder member of the Irish Horse Board, which was set up to look after the interests of the non-thoroughbred industry, and Thady travelled around the world on behalf of the Board promoting the breed.

He was also honored as an honorary life member by the Royal Dublin Society for serving over 40 years as a member, and committee member and as one responsible for many of the innovative additions to the show like the Hunt Chase, the Breeders Championship and he also was a popular commentator for the Parade of Champions, led by a different pack of hounds each year.

For many years he was an active member of the Limerick Show Committee.

Retirement

Thady Ryan retired to his wife Anne's home country of New Zealand as he had promised her, in consideration of supporting him during his career hunting the famous pack in Ireland. But he was intent on keeping up his breeding interest of Irish horses in New Zealand, so he shipped out an Irish Draught stallion Kingsway Diamond by King of Diamonds and two fillies, Kilmanagh Banrion and Night Errand. Thady made the stallion available mainly through artificial insemination to local breeders. On the flight to New Zealand their two terriers Chilli and Chips travelled in the hold of the plane. Thady remarked afterwards that it must have been the only hunt ever to take place at 35,000 feet, as one of the terriers chewed his way through the side of the kennel to get at a consignment of 300 pedigree Angora rabbits that were also travelling in the hold in a wire container. Needless to say their early education came into play, and on arrival at Christchurch there was a bit of tidying up to be done in the hold, as Chilli had dispatched a couple of the large rabbits and dined well in flight!.

He hunted occasionally in Australia with the Oakland Hounds outside Melbourne, and was the guest speaker at their Centenary Dinner. However he missed the fox who is one of the species that does not inhabit New Zealand, and the hare although he admired it, was really no substitute.

I had the privilege of staying with him briefly at his home in Timuka, in South Island, New Zealand not far from Christchurch, and although in ill health he continued to be an entertaining storyteller. After dinner he asked me when I was passing the butter knife to him if I knew that the definition of a gentleman was, 'A person that uses his butter knife, even when he is dining on his own'!

Thady continued to judge at a number of horse shows in New Zealand and Australia, and judged hounds at various packs in both countries as well as in America. But he liked nothing better than to judge at the small packs in County Kerry and County Cork.

Sadly Thady Ryan passed away at his home in New Zealand in 2004.

Michael Dempsey

Michael Dempsey is known throughout the world of hunting as the joint master and former huntsman of the Galway Blazers Foxhounds. He also hunted the Bermingham and North Galway, and the East Galway Foxhounds.

An exceptional horseman for his stature, he was known to ride possibly a number of stone lighter than his true weight. As a result he was always easy on his horses, until he sounded 'Gone Away' on his hunting horn.

He won point to point races, and once jumped two old solid railway crossing gates off the road at the back of Craughwell Village in order to stay with his hounds who were running a fox across the railway tracks.

Michael Dempsey would be considered by those who are close to him as a very modest man, and keeps his achievements very close to his chest. He is known all over the hunting world as the legendary master of the Galway Blazer Foxhounds. As Kate Horgan Chairman of the Irish Master of Foxhounds Association said at a recent AGM, "Michael Dempsey was an example to all those in hunting, and was a very special member of the Master of Foxhounds Association, and to many people around the world he is the Galway Blazers". He is just as enthusiastic about hunting today as he was over 70 years ago when he first started hunting as a 10 year old on a pony he borrowed from a neighbour Mike Hynes who he says was a 'dinger', and that if the could not jump a wall, he would bank it like a goat. A simple calculation tells you that he celebrated a very special birthday recently on the day of the opening meet in Athenry. But age is in the mind, but not in

Dempsey's, as he is as busy now as ever and does the work of many men, maintaining the Galway Blazers as the premier pack of foxhounds in Ireland. His success formula is to look after the farmers, and make sure the followers respect the country that they hunt over, and understand and appreciate the privilege it is to be allowed to ride over other people's land, and he is not slow in handling any situation that jeopardizes those principles. He has been exceptionally kind to young people who have the same passion for hunting as himself, and would go out of his way to help them by getting them mounted, and checking on their progress. In one instance a young lad was hunting bareback using a long rope reins normally used when driving a horse and cart. He had him call to him that evening and organised a proper leather reins, and also an old saddle to get him started with no charge, much to the lad's delight.

The Galway Blazers are reputed to have earned their name when during a function in Dooley's Hotel in Birr many years ago, the hotel burned down during the night as a result of the boisterous festivities. Another theory is that it was due to the popularity of dueling by the upper classes in society in the 18th century, as it became one of the ways that gentlemen settled disputes. As these were the very same people that foxhunted in Galway, duelling also became known as 'Blazing'.

Hunting Hounds

He has had an amazing fulfilled life, worked in farming, forestry, quarrying, mining and is also a much sought after show hunter judge. He hunted three different premier packs of hounds, the Bermingham and North Galway Foxhounds with Lady Molly Cusack-Smith, the East Galway with Charlie Bishop and Tim Gwynn Jones with current Blazers joint master Shirley North whipping in to him. In 1978 he took over the Galway Blazers as master and huntsman. He has made many friends in different parts of the world through hunting and through his dealing and judging of horses.

Born and reared at Dunsandle between Loughrea and Athenry beside the large estate formally owned by Blazer Master and Huntsman Major Bowes Daly, he took every opportunity to get out hunting and decided as a child that he would someday hunt the Galway Blazers. Daly was his idea of the complete huntsman, a big man that could trot a horse down to the biggest double wall in Galway and make nothing of it. He had a wonderful voice and was fantastic on the hunting horn. Dempsey's early years were spent hunting and point to pointing, but when out hunting he was always riding up front, as he knew the country like the back of his hand. For a man of large stature he was known to ride at least three stone lighter as he was such a good rider, and many of his horses would still be fit and sound enough to hunt hounds up into their late teens. His best horse was Superman who he hunted hounds off, and also won a point to point on him in Athenry. He was one of two horses that he bought from the Blake family in Tynagh, the other horse was sold for eventing to Italy. Another was Gavroche that he bought from his brother Paddy.

Horsemanship

The stories of Dempsey's skill as a rider are numerous. Hunting at the back of Craughwell one day his hounds were running strong on a good fox from Greenhouse. When he got to the railway gates they were closed as a Galway train was coming through, but Dempsey disliked being separated from his hounds, and to the astonishment of the followers and the waiting cars he took on the double of railway crossing gates foot perfect, that in those days were vertical, unbreakable and high, with just two strides complete with railway track in the middle. Needless to say nobody followed.

Another day he was visiting the Meath Foxhounds with a horse that never saw a ditch before. Everybody got held up by post and rails with a five foot hedge and ditch at the back. Dempsey decided that he had not travelled this far to be held up and turned his horse on the road and sailed out over it showing a clean pair of heels to the Meath followers.

At Carnmore Cross with hounds hunting hard on the Rifle Range there was barbed wire standing a few feet out from a high double wall, Dempsey spotted a place in the corner and had a go getting his horse to take off just on the right spot to give him any advantage of clearing it, and he was on his own for a while as the followers had to do a detour to get to him.

They were so late hunting on another day in East Galway that the only way they got across the country in the dark was to follow the sparks of Shirley North's horses shoes as he struck each wall on the way home. Once a year they hunted by invitation in Westport for two days stabling horses and hounds at Paddy Joe Foy's. As a prank a few of Dempsey's 'friends' removed the door of his hotel bedroom during the night, and he found himself somewhat confused as he awoke in the morning with the fine view of the hotel corridor from his bed!

Retiring as Huntsman

He continued to be a fearless man to follow across country until he had a serious accident that was to finish his career hunting hounds outside Loughrea in 1998, and after 20 seasons he handed over the hunting horn to his son Tom who was at the time whipping in to him. He was so disappointed at having to give up as huntsman, that a year later when his son hurt his ribs and was sidelined, against doctors orders Dempsey got back in the saddle and had a cracking hunt from Cartymore, having to take a check at multiple strands of wire sitting over the top of a double wall which looked unjumpable. Finbar Ryan got down off his horse to take it down but Dempsey could not wait and took it on to everyone's amazement. Another time, again coming out of retirement to hunt hounds, he was wearing a white neck brace at a meet at Newcastle, to be told later that he looked like a hunting priest in the distance!

Horsemanship is in the Dempsey family, with his huntsman son Tom having represented Ireland in junior eventing, Michael Jnr. hunted the East Galways Foxhounds, and another son Pat was often considered one of the finest horsemen in Ireland, spending much of his time competing in America and Germany.

How do you follow a lifetime dedicated to his hounds and hunting the fox. Well Michael Dempsey probably is more active now than ever as joint master. He often reminds his huntsman son Tom that he has all the pleasure, while Michael has all the pressure. The Blazers are fortunate to have Dempsey at the helm for the last 28 seasons, and he certainly has achieved his ambition from childhood that one day he would hunt the famous pack. It has been a long and rewarding journey.

Galway Blazer hounds at Athenry

George Briscoe

George Briscoe has been a master of the Tara Harriers for over 60 seasons, hunting the pack for many of those years, following in the footsteps of his father and grand father.

A dedicated man of the countryside, he has led a fulfilled life living in some of the most beautifull houses in County Meath like Bellinter House and Bective House that overlook the River Boyne famous for its salmon fishing. As a typical country gentleman he hunted during the Winter with his own pack the Tara Harriers and the Meath Foxhounds as well as visiting friends to hunt in County Cork. In the Summer he fished on the Boyne and the lakes and rivers in the west of Ireland, and went horseracing.

George Briscoe has a remarkable record in hunting, being one of the longest serving masters in the world. For the last 64 seasons since 1942 he has been Master of the Tara Harriers, and 50 seasons hunting hounds. He has also found time to assist the neighbouring pack the Meath Foxhounds for 17 seasons as Chairman of the hunt. Although he no longer rides to hounds he seldom misses a hunt. Catching up with him I asked him to look back and share some of his views on his life and on hunting .Recently he put pen to paper and published his life story so far, *The Best Of Times, Memoirs of a Countryman*.

He has led a very full life, adapting over the years to changes in farming and estate management, together with his passion for hunting, shooting and fishing. He has lived right through many interesting historic events in Irish life, from changes in the political landscape of the country, but also the memories of life living on a large country estate with the seasonal social calendar of dinner parties, hunt balls and lawn meets. It was a time before water and electricity were supplied as today as utilities, which meant lines of horses and carts drawing tons of coal to the country houses for heating and cooking, and before the advent of pumps supplying vast quantities of water from wells for personal and domestic use. He recalls the five seater toilet in the woods adjacent to his home Bellinter House which was common on the large estates in those days before running water in houses, just as the history books tell us of a similar one at the Palace of Versailles for the royal family. It was not unusual to have a number of the members of the family using the convenience, and conversing on the day's happenings at the same time! When the mayfly was up on the lakes in the west, the Briscoe's cavalcade of large caravans towed by cars would set off for camping trips to the west for fishing expeditions, but also for the Galway Races, where the family and extended families would often spend weeks pursuing their favourite pastimes.

The Briscoes also bred some good race horses, amongst them Royal Rubicon who won in England, Mary Mitsu won a listed race and was runner up in the Windsor Castle Stakes at Royal Ascot. Bay Empress won a group race, Jazz Musician was fourth in the Coventry Stakes, and Not Mistaken who was runner up before disqualification in the Cheltenham Champion Hurdle.

The Tara Harriers were originally known as the Bellinter Harriers owned by John Joseph Preston who was the son and heir of Lord Tara who founded the pack about 1750. When he died in 1870 he handed the pack over to George's grandfather Gustavus Villiers (Gussie) Briscoe who had managed Bellinter Estate. Gussie wagered a bet over dinner one night that he could ride his hunter up the long winding spiral staircase that ran from the basement up the three levels of Bellinter House all the way into the attic. But when he reached the attic his horse would not decend the steep staircase, so the horse had to be fed for 3 weeks in the attic while workmen constructed a pully structure so that the horse could be lowered down the three flights secured by ropes! His father Cecil in turn took over the pack of stud book harriers, for about six seasons until 1914 when he got a bad fall, and could never ride again. The pack was not hunted during the First World War, but Lord Randall Dunsany started a pack after the war called the Dunsany Harriers hunting the same country for about 5 years. Then Senator Bill Quirke bought Ringlestown House in the Tara country, and in 1935 asked Cecil Briscoe to restart a pack with him. They renovated the old kennels in 1935 and started hunting again. Due to the accident to his father, George had to leave school to manage the farm. Then in 1940 George was asked by Tom and Kit Cosgrave who were training a large number of point to pointers to take over the Kill Harriers hunt country to the west to Longwood. The amateur jockey Bunny Cox who later made a name for himself as a trainer used to ride most of their horses. His first cousin Lukie Massey hunted the Longwood end, and George took over as master and huntsman in 1942 on the Navan and Cavan part of the hunting country. He was joined by various joint masters to assist him in the large hunt country, and they had terrific hunting, but it often meant hacking horses and hounds long distances from 10 to 20 miles by road for his kennel huntsman Christy Dowdall, on the day before a hunt to get to distant meets. One night returning from Enfield with the pack in darkness and with weather conditions deteriorating, made worse by heavy snow showers, Dowdall saw a fox cross in front of him at a crossroads. Unfortunately for him the hounds spotted him too, and away they went hunting with great cry, and left him on his own on the road. He could hear them but could do nothing except wait, but in a short time they were miles away. To avoid suffering exposure he went home and reported the incident to George, who calmed him by saying that they would find their way back to the kennels. Hounds had not returned the following morning, or by that evening, and they were eventually found in the bottom of a deep ditch happily feeding on the carcass of a dead bullock that had been lying there for some days! Christy Dowdall spent 24 years with the Taras and was succeeded by his son Terry for 36 years, and the family tradition lives on with his daughter Sabine now the Tara's kennel huntsman.

After 1976 George took on all of the hunt country but usually managed to get out with Meath Foxhounds as well. He was often joined by his sisters Constance and Stella who was a very successful point to point rider. She was married to Lancelot Smith who farmed at Donabate. He farmed in the Summer so that he could get all his work done to hunt various packs of hounds during the Winter. Smith was joint master and huntsman in his career of the Fingal Harriers, the Galway Blazers Foxhounds, East Galway Foxhounds, Island Foxhounds and the Meaths Foxhounds. Stella's son Henry is a current joint master and huntsman of the Tara Harriers. Hunting seemed to run in the extended family as his cousin George Malcomson was joint master of the Ward Union Staghounds, and his wife Eleanor was joint master of the Meath Foxhounds. Another cousin was National Hunt jockey Aubrey Brabazon, who won a lot of races on Vincent O'Brien's top steeplechasers like Cottage Rake, who he rode to win three Cheltenham Gold Cups and two Irish Grand Nationals, as well as an Irish Cesarewitch at the Curragh. Hatton's Grace he rode to win two Champion Hurdles at Cheltenham, and an Irish Cambridge-shire also at the Curragh, and various wins on Knock Hard and Royal Tan.

Introduction to Hunting

George Briscoe's first hunt was in 1928 when he was 7 years old. It was a meet from Bellinter House with the Meath Hunt. He had a very good pony, one of the many that he had the pleasure to ride when he was a child.

In later years he recalled a meet at the Dancing Tree near Kilcock in County Meath when local farmer Derry Faulkner who also hunted with the Ward Union Staghounds organised the country for the days hunting. George was hoping that it would not be too strenuous as he had pulled a muscle in his leg, which used to go into spasm when he sat down, and despite seeking medical advice from some of the best medical consultants in the country, they were not able to cure him. They had a terrific days hunting, hounds running non stop, probably covering about 15 miles in all. After the hunt his joint master David Wilkinson invited him to have a meal before he went home. After the meal he stood up with no side affects, cured after the strenuous days hunting. Where doctors failed, hunting cured!

He hunted in many parts of the country, but liked to visit his friend Dick Dwyer in County Cork and hunt with the United Hunt. He would time it so that he could take in the Hunt Ball as well as get a few days shooting in as well. He recalls some terrific runs especially a fast hunt of about six miles from a meet at Watergrasshill with hounds accounting for their fox in the adjoining Muskerry Foxhounds country.

A proud moment was when his daughter Lorraine joined him as joint master. She married John McDowell, and they set up home nearby at Asigh Stud. Adjacent to the stud and joining the stud lands is a beautiful cut stone six span bridge over the River Boyne. One day George found engineers from the Board of Works examining it and enquiring as to what they were doing they informed him that they were deciding where they were going to put the explosive charges to blow it up, as they were concerned about insurance claims. He asked them could he buy it , and after some consideration they asked him if £60 would be a fair price. There was no need to bargain at that price, and he immediately did the deal. It is now known in the family as George's Bridge.

Favourite Horse
It is hard to pick one as he was really fortunate to ride some of the best, but one of his best was a horse called Clifton. He bought him from Barry Donoghue the former huntsman of the Ballymacad Foxhounds, who got him from Philip Reilly of Ballyjamesduff. He was a horse that took a real hold, and was built like a tank, but was equally foot perfect over the narrow banks of Cavan, or the wide 'yawners' of ditches of County Meath. More of his good hunters were bought from Willie Smith who used to make all his young horses hunting in County Meath, and the Chapman family who have been associated with the Island Foxhounds in County Wexford. Because the Wexford country consists of banks and trappy fly fences it has always been a good area to find a good horse.

Favourite Hound
His favourite hound was a black and tan hound called Major that came from
a foot pack in County Kerry. He had an equally good brother called Master.
They were fantastic scenting hounds, with rich voices when throwing their
tongues.

Hunting Hounds
He enjoyed hunting hounds, especially building up the pack, and developing
a relationship with them, which made it more pleasurable when out hunting,
as they could work together as a team. When they would over run a line he
would sit back and let them work out the line themselves, and then when
they found it they were off again. The pleasure he found almost impossible to
describe, as it is more natural to feel the satisfaction that to describe it.

He rates John Henry Senior the former huntsman of the Meath
Foxhounds as a terrific huntsman. He acknowledges the exceptional service
he has given to the hunt, and there was little that he did not know in
breeding or showing hounds, producing many winners in the ring.

The Future of Hunting
The only danger he sees to hunting at the moment are splits in packs, and
particularly over-hunting of country due to packs not working together
especially over land that has more than one pack hunting it. He emphasises
that followers have to respect farmers, and appreciate that you are their
guests, and expected to behave like guests, that is with courtesy and an
appreciation for being allowed the privilege of hunting over their land.
Unregistered packs are also a concern in some areas. The destiny of hunting
he advocates rests with those inside hunting not outside it.

After 50 seasons hunting hounds just 10 days before the committee were
to make a special presentation of a Peter Curling painting to him, he had a
bad fall off a 4 year old horse, which resulted in a broken neck and wrist.
Fortunately Dr. Austin Darragh then a master of the Meath Foxhounds was
hunting with the Taras that day, and took good care of him. After that
George found it difficult to ride a horse, as he had only limited mobility of
his neck, and his balance was affected. But that does not stop him continuing
as joint master, and following the hunt by car each day, and as you would
expect he is always in the right spot to view hounds, as his knowledge of the
hunt country is unsurpassed.

He sums up his life so far as being a great life, not a lot of money, but a lot
of fun.

Hugh Leonard

Hugh Leonard has played polo in Argentina, hunted with most of the hunting packs in Ireland, and particularly his local pack the Ward Union Staghounds. He has been a successfull jockey in point to points and at many of the major National Hunt racecourses, such as Punchestown and Fairyhouse, as well as riding and judging show horses.

While on a skiing holiday in Switzerland he was coopted onto the Trinity College University skiing team although he did not attend that college, and raced downhill against Oxford and Cambridge Universities.

Being a talented rider he is very much in demand in finding good hunters and competition horses, and also to school young inexperienced horses.

Usually when a person has hunted for over 60 seasons it is unusual to see them riding different horses every day of the week, to hunt chase and ride to hounds, and think nothing of it. Most people tend to acquire a nice armchair ride that will look after them, but not Hugh Leonard. I suppose due to the outdoor life he has led, he looks like a man 20 years younger and certainly behaves like one. Although he admits to being retired today and that horses are just a pastime, he hunts at least 3 days a week with either the Wards, Meaths or the Taras, often riding friends' horses and sorting out any problems they may have. The name of Hugh Leonard is synonymous with equine activities in Meath and indeed further afield, as he has led a remarkable life to date associated with horse disciplines of all types.

The Early Days

Hunting since he was 9 years old with the Ward Union Staghounds, playing polo for Ireland, producing show champions at the Royal Dublin Society, hunt chasing all over the country, winning numerous races on the track and point to points, and getting a little downhill skiing in for good measure continues in part to be the exciting life of Hugh Leonard. He was born at Moorestown beside Warrenstown Agricultural College, and was educated at St. Gerards in Bray, and then Ampleforth College in England where another great horseman, Scarteen master Thady Ryan was educated. The family farming was mainly cattle production, but they also kept horses for hunting, racing and polo. His twin sister Gretta and his two brothers Michael and Tim were just as enthusiastic about horses, and could not wait to get home from boarding school to get out for a day hunting with the local packs.

Hunting, Showing and Hunt Chasing

His first hunt was in 1942 on a pony called Dinky, but he was disappointed as groom Johnny Kelly was under strict instructions not to let him off the lead rein. But in time that was to change, and in the meantime there have been a number of red letter days that he can recall out hunting, one for example of a 13 mile run from Killeen to Kilcock stands out. But one of the most memorable days was when the hunting season had actually closed, when Eric Craigie was master of the Wards, and Charlie McCann was huntsman. There was an outlier stag in Beaupark who was damaging corn, so the master handpicked 10 of the best Ward riders for the job. Hugh had roughed off his hunters as he was getting ready for the polo season, but the master was confident Hugh would find a horse somewhere. He asked his groom Dessie Johnson if he thought any of the polo ponies would hunt. He picked out a green 4 year old and put it on a long rein and lunged it over a plain and then a blind ditch. Then Hugh rode her across a few ditches and said he would chance her. Little did he know that the run would last for 3 hours from Beaupark to Ratoath, running the stag to bay after a distance of 23 miles as they ran, with a 13 mile point. Three riders finished, huntsman Charlie McCann, master Eric Craigie on a horse named Leapyear, and Hugh on his polo pony. He hunted her for 3 more seasons, as well as playing polo on her, before selling her on to Lady Sharp who wanted a horse to ride side saddle. He later hunted a mare called Stella, for Colonel Manwearing of Ratoath while he was home on school holidays who proved difficult at first, but Hugh got the measure of her. She later represented Britain in the Olympic Games in Helsinki in 1952 ridden by Bertie Hill.

Nat Galway Greer who produced some of the finest champion hunters at the Royal Dublin Society Show used to send most of his difficult horses to Hugh to be schooled. One of the best show horses that Hugh produced was called Romeo, a grey dapple by Rondo, who he sold to Sebastian Ferranti, who hunted him for years with the Cheshire, and won numerous point to points on him in England. The other was a horse that was second out of a class of believe it or not sixty three, in the Middleweights at the Royal Dublin Society, that he sold on to South Africa and was renamed Zulu. They all had two things in common, bone and substance. He sold a horse that was third in the Heavyweight Class in Dublin to Norman Richards who said to Hugh when he met him at the RDS the following year, to call him immediately when he had another one like it. For a number of years now Hugh continues to be first choice for the Wards Union Staghounds Hunt Chase Team, competing with considerable success, and winning a number of the provincial events, as well as the team chase in the RDS.

Race riding

Hugh rode in his first point to point at the age of 17 years in Culmullen. He was given a difficult thoroughbred horse by his father, and proceeded to hunt him twice a week and ride him 3-4 hours per day. He eventually got to the bottom of him, and went on to win four point to points, and was runner up over Fairyhouse and Punchestown. The horse was later sold to trainer Dan Moore. He later went on to win 3 times for Arthur Stevenson in England. He then won 4 point to points on a mare called Mollie Brant by Hycintus, running second in the Levins Moore to Silver Drop ridden by Dr. Paddy Stokes who was sent up that year as favourite for the Aintree Grand National. Due to his success on the track, he was then offered outside rides from a host of owners like Barney Lawless, Standish Collen, Joe Moorehead and Tom Cosgrave, and won a number of races, like the Peter Simple Chase at Fairyhouse, the Mullacurry Hunt Chase and the Champion Hunters Chase at Navan, and was second in the La Touche at Punchestown.

Polo

There was a long tradition of playing polo in Hugh's family, as his father Jack was a keen player as well as his grandfather John who knew and played against John Watson the famous master of the Meath Foxhounds. Watson was the person credited with drafting up the first rules of polo. Hugh played the game from 1948 to 1970, and during that time he never missed selection for the Irish Team particularly during Horse Show week. He was one of the first to bring polo ponies from Argentina into Ireland in 1964, followed by importing 20 more in 1968. In Ireland he travelled around looking for small thoroughbred mares following in the footsteps of his father, who felt that mares were quicker to learn than geldings, who he considered to be stubborn, and the other advantage was that they could be bought cheaper.

One of his best wins in polo was the top low goal (under 4 goal players) turnout in England, the Holden White Trophy in Cowdray. The team consisted of Hugh, Major Ronnie Ferguson and Ian and Toby Balding. He was rated a handicap of 3 goals at the time and scored an astounding 18 goals in 8 games.

Judging Horses

Hugh describes himself as a retired farmer and has never looked on himself as a dealer, as he felt it was always difficult to make a living from horses alone. But he had lots of friends that trusted him to find a suitable horse for them. In addition he would always be buying and bringing on horses for himself. He has interesting views on choosing horses. Although he bought all types of horses, he liked horses with the potential to make 16.2 hands, on the premise that they are always easier to sell to well fed businessman with money! His father used to like horses that appeared small when you looked at them, but when you walk into them, they measure bigger than they look. He maintained that often a horse can seem small at first glance if he is deep set in stature. Hugh also pays particular attention to a horse's head and ears, which often signals his outlook and his attitude to his work. He has advice for anybody buying big horses. He advises them never to buy a big horse that can't turn in a tight circle. I was interested in his views on warmblood horses, and I was not surprised that he is not fond of them. He cites a number of reasons, like he feels that they lack stamina, and they lack temperament, but he does agree that they can jump. He also feels that they are not suitable as riding horses or for hunting.

When I asked him what was the most unusual sale he ever made, he felt that there were many, but one stands out in particular. An Egyptian Troop buying mission was over in Ireland headed by a Colonel Kahliffa, and they bought a number of showjumpers for their professional riders. When they came to Hugh they liked three other horses that he had, so they bought them. But in addition to selling the horses he sold them two racing pigeons and a greyhound as well! It transpired when they started schooling the consignment that one of the horses that he sold them as a hack turned out to be a better jumper than the showjumpers, and cost a lot less.

As modest as ever Hugh's adrenaline rush was and is in speed, whether racing, polo, hunt chasing or hunting. He had no wish to boast, but for some reason that he could not explain, he said he was fearless on any horse. But he reckons the real adrenaline rush is in downhill skiing, as the risk riding a horse is divided between the horse and the rider, whereas in downhill skiing is up to the skier alone, so there is nobody else to blame and therefore no excuses. He did have the pleasure while on holidays one time of representing

Trinity College against Oxford and Cambridge in a downhill race. Although he did not attend Trinity he was in the right place at the right time, and was known to be the right man for the team. The stories of Hugh's life are numerous and apparently are not over yet by a long shot. Will this man ever slow down!

Galway Blazer hounds at Loughrea

Pat O'Brien

It is remarkable how dedicated hunt staff are to hunting. Pat O'Brien joined the Tipperary Foxhounds to work in the kennels when he was 16 years of age without having any experience of riding horses. After one year he had a crash course in riding and was appointed as second whipper in. Some 40 years later he retired as huntsman of this famous pack.

He hunted with many of the household names in racing, like Willie Carson, Greville Starkey, Timmy Hyde, Aidan O'Brien, 'Mouse' Morris, P.P. Hogan and Edward O'Grady to name but a few.

He has many interests to keep him busy in retirement like greyhound racing, pony racing and following the Tipperary Gaelic hurling teams.

The Tipperary Foxhounds have a unique record of staff loyalty over the history of the pack that was founded in 1820. Being the only pack in Ireland hunting four days a week, it means a seven day a week commitment for its kennel and hunt staff particularly during the hunting season. People like Tommy Ryan worked in the kennels and whipped in from 1922 to 1958 a total of 36 seasons. Mickey Flanagan served in the same capacity from 1947 to 1991 in all 44 seasons. The present huntsman Pat O'Brien who has served under five different huntsmen and many more masters, was promoted five years ago to the role of huntsman having worked in the kennels and whipped in for much of that time to the present day. But sadly last season O'Brien announced that he was retiring at the end of the season after 40 seasons with the Tipperarys. As joint master Paul Ronan remarked "Pat O'Brien has worked for the Tipperarys for 40 seasons under many different bosses, and has

'A Photographic Year'

of Equestrian Photo-Journalist Noel Mullins

Aidan O'Connell showing Suave at the RDS Show   (Courtesy of John Minoprio)

The Galway Blazers meet at Loughrea

Kevin Donohoe Huntsman of the Ballymacad Foxhounds showing hound at the IMFA Hound Show in Stradbally

Kevin McGuinness and the Author in Makeup on the Lassie film set.   *(Courtesy of Sheila Mullins)*

Master and Huntman of the Killinick Harriers John Stafford sits tight

Total concentration at the IMFA Show in Stradbally

The door is too low for John O'Keefe's horse at Dore's Pub hunting with the County Limerick.

Kieran Cosgrave Huntsman of the Drumlin 'Calling a taxi'

Cronan Kennedy of the Ormond Foxhounds over wire

County Limerick hounds in concentration with their Huntsman Will Bryer

Drumlin Hounds followers at their new Kennels

Willow the terrier tries to distract the Meath Foxhounds at the IMFA Show at Stradbally

No problem for National Hunt jockey Paul Carberry

The Tara Harriers Hunt crossing Asigh Bridge

East Down Foxhounds Master Craig Caven on his Irish Draught hunter

Mr. Stewart's Cheshire Hounds followers led by Master Bruce Miller in Unionville, Pennsylvania, USA.

Carrig O'Reilly and Lar Sheeran at full gallop in The Phoenix Park, Dublin, Ireland

Paddy Nielson, Russell Jones and Bruce Miller Autumn hunting with Mr.Stewart's Cheshire Hounds in Unionville Pennsylvania, USA.

Graham Beere and Ken O'Reilly playing in the President's Cup, Phoenix Park, Dublin.

Larry O' Mahony President of the All Ireland Polo Club.

Nina Carberry (nearest camera) winner of the La Touche Cup at Punchestown jumps Ruby's Double

Michal Niedzialski at North Galway Point to Point

County Louth Foxhounds Masters Ralph Hoey, Gerry Boylan, Joe Callan and Edmund Mahony with the host of the Beaulieu Meet Gabriel Konig

The Bree Foxhounds apre-hunt hospitality at Jack Murphys.

Stuart Lynch Huntsman of the Goldburn Beagles

Duhallow Foxhounds parading at the RDS Show L to r Rory O'Brien, Maurice O'Connor, Michael Buckley, Ger Withers and Kate Jarvey.

Fionna Fitzgerald-Lyons riding the Gentleman's Club Bear Necessity at the RDS.

Galway Blazer's master Shirley North at Athenry

Chris Ryan master of the Scarteen Hounds and the first member of the Hunting Association of Ireland being congratulated by Gavin Duffy.

Mary O'Neill, Geraldine Dowling, Galway Blazers Master Michael Dempsey and Rosie O'Neill at Loughrea.

Declan Feeney Huntsman of the East Down Foxhounds shows his winning rosettes at the IMFA Show at Stradbally.

The Author and actor Peter O'Toole on the Lassie film set. (Courtesy of Sheila Mullins)

Tom MacGuinness riding Justa Moment at the RDS Show.

Ivan Dowling huntsman of Mr.Stewart's Cheshire Hounds in Pennsylvania riding On The Bluff.

*George Watson Master and Founder of the Melbourne Hounds with whips Danny Callinan and
Martin Rice.* *(courtesy of the Melbourne Hunt)*

*Showjumper Gabriel
Slattery jumping hedge
with North Galway
Foxhounds.*

Kay Hennessey taking a ditch in style with the Killinick Harriers

always adapted to each one of them, and fully supported them. He is an extremely popular man, and is known to have a good word for everybody, and has never made an enemy in all that time". Indeed O'Brien is a unique man in many ways. Even after all this time he arrives at a meet with a big smile, and a greeting for everybody, enthusiastic about his hounds and hunting. He is a great advertisement for hunting in the farming community, being a former Gaelic hurler and handballer. He says the last thing he talks about to a farmer is hunting. He talks of the county and club hurling, handball, point to pointing, pony racing, greyhounds and then maybe hunting! He has a special way of communicating with farmers in his strong Tipperary accent that is full of sincerity, and consequently they always have a welcome for him and his hounds. People look forward to hunting with O'Brien and he looks forward to hunting with them. He considers people like 'Mouse' Morris, Timmy Hyde and the late PP Hogan as some of the best riders to cross country in his time. He also remembers top flat jockeys like Greville Starkey, and particularly Willie Carson who always counted the hounds in couples like a professional huntsman as they were unboxed at a meet.

A Lifetime in Hunt Service

One of a family of seven born in Rosegreen, his brothers John and Jim worked in trainer Vincent O'Brien's racing stables at Ballydoyle. He got started with the Tipperary Foxhounds when Tom Neville asked him if he would drive the tractor at 16 years of age in 1966, and he spent one year collecting fallen stock, and got to know all the farmers. Promoted to second whip with Mickey Flanagan as first whip the following year, he had to take a crash course in horse riding before spending the following 8 seasons whipping in to Captain Evan Williams who rode Royal Mail to win the 1937 Aintree Grand National. He then whipped into Arthur Ryan for 2 seasons. Following that he whipped into Michael Higgens for 19 seasons still as second whip and George Hyatt for one season. On Flanagan's retirement O'Brien was promoted as first whip to huntsman Simon Probin. He was finally rewarded with the position as huntsman six seasons ago, and has lead the field with distinction. His son Paul will keep the family name flying as he is huntsman of the Kilmoganny Hounds.

Hunting four days a week is a demanding job. Managing 58 couple of hounds that have to be exercised every day, mucked out and fed. That done the country has to be arranged by travelling all around a large geographic area, which stretches from Ballintaggart in the north, south to Ardfinnan, west to Cappawhite and east to Mullinahone to meet with farmers, getting an understanding of where stock are out, and fields to be avoided. There may be fencing to be fixed and earths checked. Willie McGrath has been a tremendous help to O'Brien especially with covert management.

There is no let up in the Summer either, as they are continuously building hunt fences to overcome the increasing amount of wire fences, and of course there is whelping and looking after the young entry. It is also a time of year to travel to the various hound shows and collect his quota of red rosettes. He had no favorites hounds, but would trust one more than another, in particular Billow a bitch that is very steady and particularly good to hunt a fox on the road.

They usually breed about 7 to 8 different lines of hounds that are not too racy, but have good scenting ability. They still maintain the old County Carlow Foxhounds ST line from the days when Mrs. Olive Hall was master, and this season they have added lines from the Cottesmore, Portman, Cheshire Forest and Vale of the White Horse. He has used some of the Waterford Old English hounds successfully to improve the voice in his pack. He considers former master and huntsman Michael Higgens and Captain Evan William who won at Peterborough with Grizzle and Growler as the best hound breeders and horsemen which he has had the privilege of working with. Higgens often tells the story of one very warm morning they were coming back from hunting and decided to get a drink to quench their thirst at a local pub. As they walked into the pub the owner asked Pat what he would like to drink, and then continued by asking what his father would like!

Treakle was his best horse bought from the Kennedys of Killinaule and another horse Mountaineer who was a specialist wire jumper.

Showjumping and Racing
Always interested in Pony Racing and showjumping, O'Brien is very proud to say that top flat champion jockey Michael Kinnane was the first to ride a winner of a pony race for him. But it is with the breeding of pony showjumpers that he has achieved most success, particularly with the 14.2 hands grey mare Twylight Flight ridden by Billy Moroney. Shane Hassett is another good rider that has also ridden some of his ponies.

Retirement
A couple of seasons ago when trying to stop hounds going onto the main road towards Ballydoyle, his horse slipped from under him and pinned his leg momentarily. Replacing the bridle that had come away in the fall, he remounted and rode on for two hours, not noticing until afterwards when he removed his britches that part of his kneecap was torn away from his leg. It was stitched back successfully, but it made him reassess the situation, and decided that why spoil a good innings as huntsman so he retired after 40 enjoyable years in hunt service.

O'Brien would say "What Retirement"! He has a wide range of interests, from the Tipperary Gaelic Hurling Team, greyhounds, showjumping, and he has promised to visit and hunt with other packs as his job has been too demanding to allow him to do it up to this.

But what will Pat O'Brien miss most about hunting. Unquestionably it will be his pack of hounds, that he has bred over the years. He would remember every detail of their lives, having selected each hound's parents, making sure they could transfer to their progeny the very best voice, drive and conformation. He nurtured them since they were puppies, sending them out to the puppy walkers, visiting them to make sure that they were being treated well, and then getting them back for the annual puppy show and Autumn hunting. He would have watched their progress during hound exercise, and ensured that they were mannerly in kennels and on the hunting field. There would be many hours treating them for minor injuries, and developing that very special bond with them that hunting poet Stanislaus Lynch called, 'the invisible thread'. He would have had many occasions to celebrate with them, complementing them on the good hunting days and consoling them when they tried hard but scent was poor.

It is difficult to leave all that behind, but that is the way that huntsmen are, and at some stage they have to call it a day, but for sure they are left with special memories like no other vocation in life.

Michael Higgens, Pat O'Brien and James O'Donnell of the Tipperary Foxhounds

Rosemary Skrine

Foxhunting and producing young horses has been a way of life for Rosemary Skrine since her family moved to Ireland over 50 years ago. Her parents were both masters of hounds, and her father hunted packs both in Ireland and England.

She is one of the most knowledgeable persons on hunting, having managed a kennels and bred a pack of hounds, as well as being a master of hounds herself.

For nearly 40 years she has been honorary secretary of the Island Foxhounds, and was known to hunt every day of the week often on young horses that she had trained herself. She has bred winners in the showring on both sides of the Irish Sea, especially Magnifire the Champion 4 Year Old, Middleweight and Supreme Champion of the Royal Dublin Society Show in 2006. She has judged at most of the prestigious shows in Ireland, England and France, and has been honoured for her services to the Irish horse by the Equestrian Federation of Ireland, the Pony Club Society and the Irish Masters of Foxhounds Association.

When one thinks of the Island Foxhounds, the name Rosemary Skrine comes immediately to mind. She has been honorary secretary of the hunt since 1967, almost a remarkable 40 years, and although retired from riding now she has only missed about 7 days hunting through injury during that time. Another unique record is that she has hunted in 65 consecutive opening meets since she started hunting. Her first hunt was in a basket saddle on Mary, a 25 year old pony, when she was only 6 years with the Old Berkeley Hunt. Her memories are of beautiful hunting country made up of two sections, the valleys of the Vale of Aylesbury, and the Uplands, with its massive wooded areas. Although school sometimes got in the way of hunting, she got out on weekends on her pony Mint Tea, who was a frequent winner on the show circuit winning the Show Pony Championship at Olympia Show in 1934. She rode in a lot of competitions as a child, particularly a succession of show pony winners for Lady Hunlock.

Moving to Ireland

Rosemary Skrine was born in Hertfordshire in England, but has spent all her adult life living in Ireland producing young horses, hunting, point to point riding, show jumping, showing and holding various positions in the Pony Club. Hunting was in the family, as her father Major Stanley Barratt was master of the Romney Marsh for 2 seasons, and the Old Berkeley for 18 seasons as master and huntsman. Her mother Gloria acted as field master. Rosemary whipped in to her father, and ran the kennels which included the fallen stock collection service when her father was away on Army duty. When he got back on weekends, Rosemary used to drive his hunter in a trap to the meets, with her mother's hunter and her own behind, followed by the full pack of hounds. They later moved to the Pytchley Foxhounds as followers, before moving over to Ireland in 1950. When the family moved into Coollatin House, in County Wicklow her father took on the Coollatin Foxhounds with Lady Fitzwilliam. The pack was later known as the Shillelagh and District Hounds with Rosemary taking up the mastership and also whipping in to Fred Archibold. She was just 22 years old at the time, and she was excited about living in Ireland, as it was something new, and while she was hunting she was happy. When moving from England Rosemary's father shipped over thirteen horses and ponies that coincidentally were all originally Irish bred, that they bought from various well known dealers in England at the time like Horace Smith, Bill Manning, Oliver Dickson and particularly Jack Bamber in the north of Ireland who used to buy at all the fairs, and ship boatloads of horses to England. After a number of enjoyable seasons with the Coolattan they moved to Ballynoe in County Carlow, and Major Philip Profumo took over the mastership of the Coollatin. She remembers her father as a passionate huntsman and one of the very best to blow the hunting horn.

Hunting in Carlow

In Carlow they joined the Carlow Foxhounds now disbanded since the 1960's whose master was the well known hound breeder Mrs. Olive Hall, known affectionately as 'Missus'. Missus was a friend of the British Royal family, and occasionally was a house guest of the 10th Duke of Beaufort at Badminton in the Cotswolds in England. He was a keen breeder of foxhounds, and kept one of the outstanding and most professionally run kennels in Britain. One morning when arriving down for breakfast Missus passed a young female house guest and addressed her by saying, "Good morning Margaret ". The young person replied, "Excuse me Missus, but I am Elizabeth". Missus looked closely at her and said, "So you are, I keep getting the two of you mixed up, you look so alike". The young lady was none other than the current British Monarch, Queen Elizabeth II. Rosemary recalls many exciting days hunting, but one in particular stands out, which was a run from Killanure to Hacketstown which was 15 miles as hounds ran, over the very best of banks, ditches and walls in the county. She usually hunted five days a week with the Island, Wexford and Carlows, often on her favourite big heavyweight hunter Aubin by Ruby Port, that she was given for nothing as he was considered unridable. To get the better of him initially she hunted him 5 days a week, and he went on to win many hunter classes in the ring as well as carrying her hunting for 10 seasons.

Wexford and Producing Horses

As a horse breeder and producer she has sold horses to America Spain, France and many to Great Britain. Most of her horses were homebred or bought as 3 year olds in the field, and she broke and hunted them eventually producing them as hunters, eventers, showjumpers or for showing. Tombreen was bought in England and became Champion Novice Horse at Peterborough and followed it by winning two Championships at Tinahely and Carlow Shows. He was not shown in Dublin as she had had no proof he was foaled in Ireland. Ballymena, bought from Oliver Dickson was Champion Broodmare in Dublin, and was Champion Hunter Trials Mare in Great Britain. She was bought for £20 as a 4 year old, and had 6 foals of which 3 were Dublin winners. They were all by Ruby Port. Another horse Mandoran won the In Hand Championship in Dublin. Paradise Walk was evented by International eventer and former Tipperary Foxhounds master and huntsman Michael Higgens, before going to Major Eddie Boylan who rode him in the European Championships. Unfortunately he was fatally injured competing at Badminton having already been shortlisted for the Irish Olympic Team. Rubena, homebred by Ruby Port was another eventer ridden by Michael Higgens. She produced Tiger Man that she bought as a yearling from George Chapman who became one of the best horses to hunt hounds off.

Rosemary got married in 1960 to Charlie Skrine who was master and huntsman of the Wexford Foxhounds before the war, a keen point to point rider, whose family were lifelong members of the Island Foxhounds. He was a Commander in the Royal Navy. They were only married for 6 years when Charlie passed away when Rosemary was reading a letter to him sitting on the sofa at home. By that time they had a family, their son David who now manages the family farm, and Susan who is married to British Olympic event rider Tiny Clapham's eldest brother Stephen. Rosemary picked up the reins in the Island Pony Club, and took over as hunt Honorary Secretary succeeding her late husband, to span three generations of the Skrine family holding the office. Starting with her father in law Walter who was appointed in 1910, Charlie then succeeded him, and Rosemary took up the office in 1967 to the present day, spanning nearly 100 years in the same family.

She plans to continue breeding from the line of her last broodmare Varina who is by Varano that stands at Paddy Byrne's Park House Stud in Co Carlow. She had five colts and one filly. The combination of the Canadian thoroughbred stallion Tasset originally owned by Sheikh Mohammed, now standing at David Murphy's Clohamon Stud and her mare Varina produced perhaps the breeder's greatest show success. The progeny is the gelding Magnifire who won the 4 Year Old Championship, the Middleweight Championship and the Supreme Championship of Dublin Horse Show in 2006. Rosemary has held on to a two year old full brother and a yearling full sister of the champion.

Judging and Awards

As a show judge she has judged at shows in Ireland, Limogue in France, and at various show hack societies, as well as the Royal International, East of England and Royal Windsor Shows. She was awarded the Equestrian Federation Medal of Honour presented to her by the then President of Ireland Mary Robinson, which made for a double celebration as Rosemary was a great admirer of the President whose mother hunted with the North Mayo Harriers.

She joined the Old Berkeley Pony Club in 1929 where her mother Gloria was District Commissioner, and continued her involvement in Ireland by holding various positions such as District Commissioner and Instructor, representing Wexford, Waterford and Kilkenny, and is currently Vice Chairman and a Board Director. For her extraordinary contribution to the Pony Club she was awarded the Carew Medal in 1990.

She has also judged at Foxhound Shows, and the Irish Master of Foxhounds Association made a special award to her for her services to hunting.

Island master George Chapman describes Rosemary Skrine as "Absolutely loyal to the Island Foxhounds, and is there to guide the members with the benefit of her years of hunting experience". She has no intention of retiring, as Chapman says "The members would be very disappointed if she did retire". She loves hounds, and is always to be seen at the right vantage points at every meet. Otherwise she is chatting to farmers enquiring about their families, while at the same time keeping an eye on her beloved Island Hounds.

Eamonn Dunphy

Eamonn Dunphy started working in the Laois Foxhounds Kennels when he was 14 years of age. After gaining his initial kennels experience he was appointed whipper in to the Kildare Foxhounds under the well known huntsman Jack Hartigan who was a renowned breeder of hounds. He enjoyed showing his hounds during the Summer, and was an expert horseman across the Kildare hunting country in the Winter.

In 1966 Eamonn got the opportunity to hunt the Ward Union Staghounds, a position he was to occupy for 25 seasons, ending when he had a serious fall from a horse. But there was to be continuity in the family as he handed over the hunting horn to his nephew Pat Coyle, who continues the family tradition.

Hunt followers continue to be fascinated by all those committed men and women who give their whole working lives to hunt service, totally dedicated to horses, hounds and the countryside. They are a unique species in this day and age. One such dedicated person who started working in hunt service at 14 years of age was Eamonn Dunphy the retired huntsman of The Ward Union Staghounds.

Eamonn was born near Durrow in County Laois where his father Ned who he refers to in admiration as 'A mighty man', was a small farmer and supervisor in the forestry, drawing timber from the nearby woods with Clydesdale and Irish Draught horses. It was here that Eamonn got his first love of horses, but he also acquired a knowledge from his grandfather of treating animals with natural medicines, that were made from locally grown herbs. He used to drive him around to farms in a pony and trap when farmers called on his help for their sick animals. As he recalls some lived and more died.

Laois Foxhounds

His first job was with the Laois Foxhounds doing general work around the kennels which was convenient as it was near his home, when Captain H.C.P. Hamilton was master. Paddy Shanahan who was later to go on to hunt the Fingal Harriers for close to 40 seasons was first whip, and John Lawless exercised the horses. His father came home from work one day with a newspaper that a fellow worker had wrapped his lunch in, where by accident he saw an advertisement for a second whips job with the Kildare Foxhounds. So encouraged by his mother Sis, he applied for the job at 14 years of age. He was promptly interviewed by the joint masters Major and Mrs. Beaumont, who were delighted to find a suitable person locally.

Kildare Foxhounds

Now on the first rung of the ladder in real hunt service with a new job and an increase in wages, he spent the following three years as second whip building up his hunting experience before promotion to first whip, a position that he was to occupy for a further 11 seasons to the famous huntsman Jack Hartigan, who he affectionately describes as like another father to him. Joe Lenihan was then appointed to fill his position as second whip. Hartigan he refers to as a 'fierce hound man' consistently winning red rosettes, particularly at the National Hound Show. He was very quick to get through the country, always letting the hounds do the work. But he could lift or carry hounds who were wrong on a line without anybody noticing. Like Hartigan, the Kildare followers liked to see hounds working, they were patient when hounds were drawing, and understanding of the difficulties of hunt staff on poor scenting days. Dunphy recalls followers at the time like Stan Cosgrave, Pat Taffee, Joe Osborne, Maxie Cosgrave, John and Deidre de Burgh, Bobby Coonan, Paddy Kerr and Ali Moore, all as he says were 'mighty people'.

The Kildares had a unique system for Covert Keepers, who got a bonus if a fox was found in their covert, and another bonus for the run, as long as he did not go to ground in their area. Hartigan kept the records, and they called to collect their money every month. Consequently regular runs of over an hour were common. They hunted officially 4 days a week, but they usually put in a bye day to make it 5 days. They ran a tight breeding policy, using the best stallion hounds available and entering more than 30 couple of new entry each season.

Dunphy recalled the famous hunt from the Kennels a few weeks after the master Major Beaumont died. He had lived in Harristown, near Two Mile House. Hounds found as soon as they entered Brophy's Covert at Herbertstown near the house. As hounds ran they crossed by Two Mile House and over the Dublin to Kilcullen road and on up Silliott Hill scaling the demense wall of Harristown Estate as their cry increased coming up through the woods. Suddenly hounds stopped in their tracks at the graveyard where the Major was buried the previous week, after a 50 minute run. Nobody has ever been able to explain it. Hartigan tried casting in every direction but could not pick up the line. It remains a mystery to this day, why the hounds stopped beside the grave of their former master Major Michael Beaumont, without a sighting of a fox.

The Ward Union Staghounds

In 1966 after eleven seasons as first whip to the Kildares, Jack Hartigan suggested he apply for the vacancy as huntsman of The Ward Union Staghounds, and he was interviewed and appointed. Charlie McCann who was hunting hounds was busy with other farming interests at the time. To get familiar with the country Dunphy whipped into Charlie for two seasons before taking over as huntsman. The Starter at Punchestown Hubie Tyrell reassured him that he was suitable for the job by saying that he would 'put a bit of life into the Wards'.

Andy Lynch who was later travelling head man for racehorse trainer Noel Meade, joined Eamonn as honorary whip as well as helping in the Kennels. The work was hectic looking after horses, hounds and over 100 deer. They always had 40 to 50 stags fit to hunt. Dunphy would walk down through them on a Sunday afternoon and pick the stags for the following week. Local farmers would expect him to have a good deer for their area particularly the best meets which were usually at Garristown, Ratoath and The Hatchett. Taking two deer to each hunt meet, the followers could expect two fast hunts of 35 - 40 minutes on a moderate deer, and more on good deer. The Wards were mainly using draft hounds and not breeding many pups at the time, so with the assistance of Captain John and Rosemary Wentges they started building up a pure Dumfriesshire pack using the stallion hound Dumfriesshire Donovan and three Dumfriesshire draft bitches in whelp. Within a few seasons with 13 puppies in one litter alone, they had 15 couple of hounds ready to hunt. Dunphy was considered one of the very best by Captain Wentges hunting this sensitive breed of hounds. Hunts of over 2 hours were common with four deer in particular. The Kilmartin Stag, the Donoghmore Stag, the Beaupark Hind and the Bush Hind, who all guaranteed 2 to 3 hours runs.

On one occasion the Kilmartin Stag was enlarged at Ashbourne and ran to Cushinstown toward Skryne, and back to the Windmill in Garristown through Tobergraegan onto Nuttstown by Pat Rooney's and the Folly, then towards the graveyard at Oldtown. They eventually caught him at the Old Mill at Cloughertown after a run of 2 hours and 50 minutes. Archie Moore was getting married that night, and they had to lift him off the horse to get him ready for the wedding!

The Donaghmore Stag was enlarged at Johnny Ward's of Fieldstown, and he ran by Dreaper's Gallops to Donaghmore and on to Ashbourne all the way to the Hill of Painstown where they took him after 3 hours. Three masters were left behind leaving Philip O'Connor to act as temporary field master. Dunphy has special mention for Larry Rowan and 'Pudser' Toole who whipped into him, and went on to be two of the most popular masters of the Wards.

Sadly Dunphy's hunting career came to an end as a result of an unfortunate accident when hunting outliers after the season was over. His horse stepped into roots while cantering, and both horse and rider were brought down with the horse rolling on Dunphy, resulting in him spending 16 weeks in hospital with a broken pelvis and other internal injuries, spending the time confined in a plaster cast. Fortunately Liam Carey found him in time. He tried to come back to hunt the hounds, but in the end handed over the hunting horn after 25 seasons to his nephew Pat Coyle, who had whipped into him.

Motorways, wire and traffic have changed the country, and he has the greatest respect for his nephew Pat and all huntsmen who have to contend with these new intrusions into the countryside.

Today Dunphy still plays an important role in the Ward Union, acting as caretaker in the Kennels, as well as occasionally following his favorite meets.

He feels fortunate that he has two women behind him, his wife Lelia and their godchild Tara. I asked him what his favourite saying was, and his reply was, "Mine's a Jameson", that is the Irish whiskey type, but he points out that he has to be careful that his wife does not hear him!

John Pickering

John Pickering came to Ireland as whipper in to the Bermingham and North Galway Foxhounds when the legendary Lady Molly Cusack-Smith was master and huntsman. He remembers his first meeting with Lady Molly at her home in Bermingham House when she was standing at the top of the long winding staircase smoking a cigar. He is one of the most jovial of people, and was very popular with the hunt followers for his charm and wit.

He has a sharp memory for hunting stories, and having started working in hunt service in County Galway he went on to hunt three other packs of hounds in Ireland before returning to Galway to hunt the pack again. He since has retired to live in the west of Ireland town of Tuam.

John Pickering has always represented the true spirit of hunting, and is a great storyteller and good company to be with. He is a former huntsman of the East Down Foxhounds, the Golden Vale Foxhounds, the Oriel Harriers and most notably whipper in and huntsman to the late and legendary Master of the Bermingham and North Galway Foxhounds Lady Molly Cusack-Smith. I first met him when he was hunting the Oriel Harriers in the 1980's. At a meet north of Dundalk, County Louth hounds put a fox away from Bells Covert, but he only ran a couple of hundred yards before going to ground in an earth in the middle of a field. To make matters worse his best hound Heckler was down in the foxhole with only his stern in view. Pickering sat casually back in the saddle and remarked, "I think I will have to take that hound to a shrink", "Why", I remarked, and Pickering replied, "Because he thinks he's a bloody terrier"!

Family background and Hunt Service

Pickering was born in Warwickshire where his father Howard was a farmer, and also kept hunt liveries. His mother Kathleen Holden was from County Wexford. Always having a deep love of horses and hounds he started hunting as a 9 year old with the Atherstone Foxhounds, and later with the Meynell and South Staffordshire Foxhounds, and North Warwickshire Beagles.

He joined the late Lady Molly in 1969 as kennel huntsman to her pack the Bermingham and North Galway Foxhounds, now disbanded, that she and her husband Sir Dermot founded in 1946. She had hunted the Galway Blazers from 1939 to 1943, which was 100 years after her great, great, great grand uncle John Dennis hunted the Blazers. Pickering's only previous knowledge of her was seeing articles in high society magazines describing the tall well-groomed elegant lady who was a haut couture clothes designer, accomplished singer, cordon bleu cook , and sharp-witted lady huntsman and master of hounds. He admits to having been terrified of her when he first met her, as she was peering down at him smoking a cigar standing at the top of the long winding stairs. He quickly got the opportunity to hunt the hounds, and Lady Molly used to review each day's hunting after dinner, analysing what went right and what went wrong, and getting Pickering to blow the correct calls on the hunting horn until she was satisfied. He says she was brilliant with hounds and on the hunting horn, and he learned so much from her. The first time he hunted hounds was at the opening meet. Lady Molly started blowing the hunting horn as hounds went away, but Pickering told her to be quiet declaring "I am hunting the hounds". Lady Molly responded by saying" Fair play to you Pick, you have to put your foot down with me, I respect that"! He was to continue to hunt the hounds for five more enjoyable seasons.

The East Down Foxhounds

He decided to move from Galway when offered the huntsman's job with the East Down Foxhounds, as he says he was attracted by better money and no abuse!

James Pooler, Albert Lowry, Patrick Forde and Charlie McCrumbe were joint masters, and they enjoyed great sport, and a lot of success with their hounds in the showring. They won the Ikey Bell Cup with the unentered bitch Password by Zetland Hamlet out of Passport, and made a clean sweep at the National Hound Show held in the Royal Dublin Society. They also added the Championship at Lisbellaw and Balmoral with Harker by Zetland Hamlet out of Portman Sample walked by their present joint master Craig Caven. The current huntsman Declan Feeney started hunting with him, much preferring fox hunting to school. He recalls a children's meet when they found at Russell's Bog, and ended up 3 miles from the kennels and 7 miles from the meet, with children scattered all around the countryside much to their delight.

The Oriel Harriers

In the early 1980's after six seasons with the East Down he moved as huntsman to the Oriel Harriers for two seasons with Mick Tuite and Sally Cox as joint masters. Tuite had a great relationship with the farmers so consequently they had full access to the country, and Sally the was wife of the well known trainer and former champion amateur jockey Bunny Cox, and they were very popular around the area as well. They hunted politically sensitive areas in the north of Ireland for that particular time, such as Forkhill and Crossmaglen in South Armagh. But there was a lot of support for the hunt and showjumper James Kiernan's family were very hospitable, putting on a regular lawn meet.

The Golden Vale

Pickering's next move was to the Golden Vale Foxhounds in Tipperary. He loved the country, as it was great scenting ground. A fox could be gone 10 minutes and there was no difficulty in picking him up compared to the more difficult light scenting conditions in County Galway.

He loved being with people, and the followers were always amused when people remarked that although the previous huntsman reared a large family in the house in the kennels, it was too small for Pickering's parties! Joint master Timmy Hyde hosted exceptional lawn meets, and his fellow master Michael Purcell the beef exporter were popular with the farmers. Purcell supplied Pickering with a daily cattle price list, so that as well as hunting hounds, he could also inform the farmers of Purcell's current cattle prices! Former hunting contributor to *The Irish Field* Colin Lewis gave Pickering a few bottles of a homemade cure for his sore knees, which had equal parts of poitin (Irish home brewed spirits), wintergreen and olive oil. Lady Molly drank it by mistake one evening, and afterwards when she was lighting her cigar after dinner there were anxious moments for her guests as they thought that she would blow up!

Back to North Galway

He was approached to go back in 1985 to the newly formed North Galway Foxhounds as huntsman and could not resist the temptation to get back with Lady Molly now as honorary master, with joint masters Professor James Houghton, James Storan and Dr. John Waldron.

They had good hunting, and had introduced some old hound bloodlines back into the pack through the then master and huntsman of the Westmeath Foxhounds John Smith, who managed to find six couple of hounds going back to two of Lady Molly's favorite doghounds, Planter and Godfrey. She did not like the hairy Welsh hounds and made no secret of it, and used to remark, that all they would catch was sheep and fleas!

During Galway Race week Lady Molly always had house guests, and everything was done elaborately with dinner served with the gentlemen in black tie, and ladies in evening dress amidst cocktails and candelabras. All the staff that Lady Molly employed over the years were called into action, like May McGrath, Dick Tighe, Mrs Hannon and Tom Murray. Pickering recalls that the gentleman who was assigned the job of parking guests cars was only ever known to have ridden a bicycle, and it remained a mystery how the cars remained intact!

The evening always ended with the host singing one of her favourite party pieces like The West's Awake, or The Queen of Connemara.

Retirement

Now retired and living in Tuam, Pickering passes the time helping former master of the North Galway Foxhounds Dr. John Waldron with his thoroughbred mares. He likes living in Tuam, and says that he has now qualified to be a 'Tuam Sham', which is a Tuam term for somebody who has been accepted as a local.

John Pickering with the Bermingham and North Galway Foxhounds

Maxie Scully

Maxie Scully is an inspiration to anybody who wants to achieve a goal in life, even if it seems at first as unachievable. He has had a series of setbacks to his health since he was 18 years of age, and is one of the longest recipients of a donor kidney in Ireland, having had a transplant more than 30 years ago. He has had to contend with seven heart attacks, a triple heart bypass, have cancer growths removed frequently, and has also had a tumor removed from his brain.

Despite that he has always maintained a positive attitude. He is a keen hunt follower, and an accomplished showjumper, achieving one of his main ambitions which was to establish a new World record by jumping 6 feet 7^1/$_2$ inches riding a horse bareback over poles at the Royal Dublin Society Indoor Show on the showjumping horse Drumlogan.

It's quite a humbling experience to interview Maxie Scully considering the bravery that he has shown, given all the challenges that he has had to deal with in life. Aside from his remarkable achievements in his 51 years to date, he also had to deal with a series of serious health problems, such as, seven heart attacks, a triple heart bypass, a kidney transplant, removal of a gall bladder, the insertion of a defibrillator, the removal of skin cancer growths every three months as a result of the side effects of crucial medication, removal of a tumour from his brain, and he is on a waiting list for a heart transplant in the future. The tragedies of losing his brother and sister earlier on, and the recent death of his 17 year old son Marcus in a road accident, which he is desperately trying to cope with at the moment. As he says he was so proud of him, they were good pals, and he "misses him like hell". Maxie is a remarkably focused and driven person, and is an example to anybody who has to deal with trauma in their life. Of course one has to grieve, but he also believes that one has to 'live for today', and his motto at times of despair and adversity is to think of a special occasion and say "I would like more of that". As his sister Lorraine remarked, "If he could bottle his bravery and will to live, he would be a millionaire".

Family Background

His family home was in Gort County Galway, where his mother Olga, sisters Barbara, Olga and Lorraine, and brothers Garret and Greg were surrounded by horses and talk of horses. His father Mark was an eminent Veterinary Surgeon with a gift for treating horses, one of the first vets to treat horses for brucellosis, and spent his leisure time hunting with the Galway Blazers, acting as a member of the Galway Show Committee, sailing competitively, and commentating at shows. As a permit holder he trained Lisabelle to win the Galway Guinness Hurdle at 66/1. He was also a tremendous inspiration to Maxie with the courage he demonstrated in the course of his life.

A Life with Horses

His earliest memory is as a 4 year old dressed in an Aran sweater at his first Galway Blazers meet at Tulira Castle, then the home of Lord and Lady Hemphill. He credits Lady Anne and the Galway Blazers Pony Club, with introducing him to the finer points of riding and looking after all aspects of ponies. Her memories of Maxie were "The naughtiest boy, but the greatest fun"!

His first pony was a 12.2 hand called Patience bought from Paul Tully in Castlerea, who won at all the main pony competitions around the country shows, and was 3rd at the Dublin Spring Show. The Belvedere Show was held around the corner from the Royal Dublin Society which followed the Horse Show, and on one occasion he swept the boards, winning the 13.2 and 14.2 Novice and Open events, and even the Musical Chairs! His next pony was appropriately named Red Hot who he regards as a very talented pony and was always in the ribbons. He compares winning to being like an addiction, he got such a high from it. Earning a reputation as an accomplished rider, he had no shortage of ponies to ride for other owners. He proudly recalls his good 14.2 pony Coolairne Hero beating the Paddy Griffin produced, and later the Harvey Smith ridden Hickstead Derby winner Mattie Brown in the High Stone Wall Competition in Kilcolgan. The pony was a frequent winner ridden by Maxie and his sister Olga at all the Provincial Shows, and was 6th in Dublin. His first opportunity to wear the International green blazer of

Ireland came when he was chosen on the International Pony Team to compete at the Royal Dublin Society Show in Dublin, but due to ill health Maxie had to step down.

When at boarding school in Garbally Park in Ballinasloe, he came to the conclusion that to fulfill his single ambition to ride for Ireland, and his dream of wearing the International blazer of Ireland he needed more professional coaching, and to learn the finer points of horsemanship. So he spent Easter and Summer holidays in Sligo with Frank McGarry and Francie Kearns, who he refers to as the gentleman of the showjumping circuit, as they were so kind and helpful to him. He also received coaching from Curly Beard and attended clinics by Captain Pallman in Dublin. The first sign of a breakthrough was when he was long listed for the International Junior Team, but unfortunately it was not to be.

Coming from a family that enjoyed hunting and showjumping on moderately priced horses, it was quite a different price range to buy expensive International level showjumping horses. Maxie concluded that the only way was to apply to the Army Equitation School, and was delighted to be accepted. Even though he passed the medical examination, and just before he was called for training to the Officers School in the Curragh he very suddenly lost the use of his kidneys, which was a terrible blow to his ambition, and left him devastated. The cause was a rare blood disorder called Good Pastures Syndrome, which only one in a million people survive. As a result he had to go for six hour dialysis three times a week. Fortunately he was called for a kidney transplant in 1975, and was told by his doctors that it was doubtfull if he would ever be able to ride horses again. However Maxie planned to defy the medics as he started to rebuild his fitness and his life. To have a qualification behind him he completed his Hotel Management studies to use as a backup career.

Going for the World Bareback Record and the Irish Blazer

His friend Rory Hearne former joint master of the North Galway Foxhounds asked him to join National Aluminum, which was to see Maxie getting the company involved in showjumping sponsorship through the late Paul Darragh, riding two sponsored horses National Aluminum and National Double Glazing. At the Royal Dublin Society Indoor Show in Simmonscourt he saw Johnny Coyle going close to breaking the World Bareback record, and instantly decided that he wanted the World record for Ireland. So he set about getting a suitable horse. Marlyn Dawson kindly lent him Clare Cottage, but unfortunately the horse got injured.

While assisting Call Steward Tommy Condron at the RDS Indoor Show, he saw this huge 18 hand gangly horse Drumlogen with Francie Kearns on board coming down to a box parallel all wrong, and even though he was such a big horse Kearns managed to right him in time for the fence. So immediately Maxie thought that this horse was his best chance to take the record. He described the horse as a giraffe that you could fit the whole family on his back it was so long, but very honest and genuine. Francie asked the owner John Rogers if he would agree to let Maxie have a go at the record and after some negotiation he agreed. But just before the competition, there was a problem, as Show Director Eddie Taylor said Maxie could not take part as he was concerned about his health situation. But Joan Mullins stepped in and advised Taylor that it was an open competition, and that Maxie was entitled to jump. After satisfying the Show Organisers by signing multiple health disclaimers he was free to take part. The horse had earlier won the Grade B competition, and despite Maxie not having sat on a horse since the previous July and it was now November, he had a few pops on him over small fences in the pocket and declared that he was satisfied with the horse, and that he would see everybody later. That night there was an air of anticipation in the crowd of a possible new World Bareback record. The fence started at 5 foot 8 inches and went to 6' foot $7^1/_2$ inches with both Commandant Gerry Mullins and Maxie the only riders clear. The coursebuilder fellow Galwayman Paul Duffy added half an inch and although 18 hand Drumlogan clattered a pole he realised he was clear when the commentator Tom Hudson announced 'a new World Bareback Record for Ireland'. Maxie, despite landing somewhat uncomfortably on his horse's razor-like back, had achieved his goal. To prove that it was not a once off, Maxie jumped again the following year having been called for International duty achieving his dream of a green blazer, after being earlier told that he would never ride again. Having jumped 6 foot 8 inches it was then offered at 6 ft $10^1/_2$, but the riders declined and it was put up to 7 feet. Three riders went for it, Maxie and two professionals, Michael Whitaker and Robert Smith. Whitaker got it on his third attempt. Maxie just missed the world record narrowly, but set another new Irish record. He decided in 1984 to stop showjumping but got back later riding mainly in Charity Events. At this stage he had a half share in Drumlogan, but gave the horse back to Francie to ride, and retired him some years later.

He was to have another bareback success when his novice horse King Logan, ridden by Michael Blake as Maxie had just had triple heart bypass surgery, jumped 6 feet $10^1/_2$ inches bareback in Clonshire creating a new Irish record. After his 7th heart attack he was again told that he would never ride again, so he sold the horse.

World Transplant Games
Maxie was a firm supporter of the World Transplant Games, whose aim was to show the world that transplantation can transform people, enabling them to lead active lives regardless of their abilities. He attended the foundation event as the sole Irish representative at Portsmouth in England in 1978. Competing against 99 athletes from around the world he won so many events that he was named Champion Athlete. Always one to help out, the Australian Team were short one athlete for the 4x100 relay and Maxie agreed to step in. The team won the event but were later disqualified on the grounds of Maxie not being eligible. As a Council Member and competitor he was a familiar sight at all subsequent events, in New York, Athens, Amsterdam, Budapest, Japan, Innsbruck, Singapore, Vancouver, Manchester and Nancy in 2003 where he was guest of honour, and the Council conferred him with a Lifetime Achievement Award.

Looking to the Future and the next Milestone
Maxie's life has been a series of numerous high points punctuated by huge tragedies and disappointments, but his instinct has always been to remain positive and focused on living.

Recently a friend, Julie Quinn from Wales offered Maxie a stallion named King Cotton Gold by Cavalier Royale standing 16.2 hands who was winning 1.20 metre competitions in France. He was delighted to accept the offer. After hunter trialling him on cross country courses, and hunting him with the Galway Blazers and with the Bicester, Quorn, and Beaufort Hunts in England, he has no reservation in saying that he is the best horse that he has ever owned.

So what is Maxie Scully focusing on next? Disappointed with the results of the Irish Three Day Eventing Team at the Athens Olympics he wants to compete on the team in the next Olympics in Beijing in China, and win a gold medal for Ireland. Can he do it? Well you have to say that he has a good track record when he decides to do something, and who knows, it certainly could be the icing on the cake.

Spreading the Message
Although he treats the Bon Secours and Beaumont Hospitals like his second home as a result of his need to frequent the medical teams there so often, he also is playing an increasingly important role that will benefit other patients who require donor organs. Acting as an ambassador for organ donation and transplantation, together with another well known supporter of showjumping, Anne Smurfit, his last lecture tour took him to the Ukraine, Japan and South Africa as a guest speaker at various Medical Conferences.

He wants to show people how they can get on with life, and encourage a worldwide network for the distribution of basic medicines and especially organ donation and transplantation.

Footnote

Since our interview, regrettably Maxie Scully that exceptional equestrian and strong-willed personality lost his fight for life, ironically on the day of the Puissance Showjumping Competition at the Royal Dublin Society Annual Show on the 12th of August 2006, at the early age of 52 years. There was an air of sadness as the commentator in the Main Arena reminded the spectators of the day that Maxie created a World Bareback High Jump record back in 1981 in the Royal Dublin Society, and where he had been a Steward and Commentator for over 25 years.

Keith Rankin, Emer Mullins, Fionna Lyons and Marie White at Punchestown Races

Morgan Llywelyn

Morgan Llywelyn is a best selling author, with sales of over 70 million copies of her books. Her love of horses began when she was a child, eventually leading to her competing in both showjumping and eventing.

After recovering from a serious riding accident while eventing, she turned her attention to dressage riding. Rising quickly through the grades, she went on to be short listed for the American team that represented her country in the Montreal Olympic Games, only to be relegated in the final trial to reserve, missing a place by only half a penalty point.

Saraidh Morgan Llywelyn is a lady in love with Ireland. Although born in New York and raised in America of County Clare parents, she spent almost every Summer in the Banner County of Clare. Her knowledge and library of Irish history is vast, and she also speaks the Irish language fluently. A hallmark of her life has been her ability to focus without exception on challenging goals in life, and make a success of them. Whether it has been working as a model, dance teacher or horse trainer, riding instructor, rider or as an author. In the latter she has achieved International honors. She is small in stature but big on presence; she is a welcoming, chatty and personable individual with vast energy, and is extremely happy to be living in Ireland. She has had disappointments in life, and accidents, but she has always adapted to whatever incident that has occurred positively, particularly when she had a serious fall from a horse while competing in a Three Day Event in America. But the accident although tragic at the time was to lead on to two major achievements in her life, that of being short listed for the American

Olympic Dressage Team in Montreal in 1976, and becoming a best selling author whose books have sold over 70 million copies.

Early Introduction to Horses

The family moved to Texas when she was a child. At 10 years of age she was taking time off from school to ride polo ponies at Longmeadow outside Fort Worth. It was managed by Louis Ramos who offered to teach her to ride and play polo if she mucked out the stables on the weekends. Tigie Lancaster had jumpers stabled there, and that started her show jumping, and catch riding on the South Western Circuit. When she was 15 years of age through catch money savings, and competition prizemoney she bought her first good horse, a 7 year old Anglo Arab mare Briar Rose, that she jumped and barrel raced. The combination did well in prizemoney at all the Provincial Shows.

She got married to Charles Winter who was in the American Air Force, which meant that they moved to various postings around the country. She has a fine painting in her house of Charlie, painted as the redheaded Brian Boro by artist Jim Fitzpatrick. When they moved to Colorado she taught riding at Loreto Heights College outside Denver, where their son Sean was born. After taking a break she met Lawrence Phipps who owned the Arapahoe Hunt Club and began competing at shows again, and drag hunting with the Club. But she was to have a serious fall from a novice horse when turning him over, fracturing her pelvis, arm, two legs and multiple ribs. The medics confined her to a body cast, and she had to promise her husband Charlie that she would not jump a horse again. Attending a show outside Denver she was fascinated with the performance of a black mare Starless Night with its rider wearing white tie and tails, performing a dressage routine under low lights. She was immediately determined to ride dressage, and in 1966 bought her first dressage horse who was part Appaloosa named Blue Moon. She trained her but felt she was limited, so she traded her in for another horse named Unchained Melody, a thoroughbred bought off the racecourse. Back competing in Texas she was placed 3rd first time out. Colonel Charles Valko, a Hungarian trainer agreed to train her. They won everything that was to be won in Texas. She then moved on to another military trainer Hector Carmona from Chile, and began competing in New Jersey on the East Coast of America where there were more competitions. Shortly the combination became 3rd level National Champions. The combination then had the challenge to step up to preliminary Grand Prix level.

Atticus and the Olympics

As a result of her husband Charlie's posting change she was on the move again returning to Pennsylvania stabling at Debbie Cookman's Peacefield Farm. Debbie had bought a big grey horse Atticus from Olive Watson, daughter of the founder of IBM Thomas Watson for hunting, but they found that he did not like to jump. She sold Unchained Melody to pay for Atticus who was 7/8 thoroughbred and 1/8 Canadian hunter. At their first dressage show in 1971 at York Pennsylvania, they won both main classes. They really impressed the judge Bert de Nemethy a man later to become trainer of the American Showjumping Team.

Atticus was to become the horse of a lifetime. The day of the major Dressage Show in Long Island, when wealthy Oyster Bay residents were sipping champagne and eating strawberries on the same day as Secretariat won the last leg of the Triple Crown, the wind blew the marquee down and the canvass touched Atticus as he was doing his extended trot, but he never missed a beat, putting him into number one spot. She describes the big 16.3 hand grey horse as having enormous power, $7^1/_2$ inch cannon bone, of stable disposition, unexcitable but with a brain, and absolutely unflappable. Morgan admits that it is hard to get a horse with brilliance that is unflappable, to suit her own personal highly strung nervous and twitchy disposition. When you pushed the button he came to life, and when you switched it off he relaxed. Dressage trainer Colonel Bengt Ljungquist often described Atticus as a square soft mover, with a great suspension system, no jolt or jog on any movement, even on the extended or sitting trot. The horse had received a blow of some kind to the left side of his jaw and did not like it touched there. She did a lot of work with him on the lunge line, to get his mouth properly on the bit, and his nose behind the vertical, which worked, as she proudly showed me her invitation letter to the Final Trial for the American Dressage Team for the Montreal Olympics in 1976 at Gladstone Park. She missed the team by 5/10ths of a point, and was relegated to team reserve. She blames herself for not pushing him more on the passage, as it was one of his strongest moves, but she was nervous because it was going so well and she did not take the chance. Hindsight is a great thing, she now knows that she should have gone for broke and not been so careful. There were no concessions, even though the horse and rider were good enough to make the Team. Bert de Nemethy was there as show jumping coach and her former tutor the Swede Colonel Bengt Ljungquist was managing the Dressage Team. America won the only medal they had ever won in Dressage that year, a Team Bronze. Morgan was fascinated by the Gold Medal winner Dr. Reiner Klimke on his chestnut horse Mehmed, who when he finished his round, just dropped the reins and casually did passage only using his legs. A great admirer of Dr Klimke, Morgan also studied the styles of the West German Liselotte Linsenhoff and Piaff, and former World Dressage Champions the Russian Elana Petushkova and her horse Pepei, and West Germany's Josef Neckerman and Mariano. After the Olympics Morgan travelled around the country doing exhibition dressage on Atticus.

A Change of Direction

To distract her from her disappointment her mother got her to research the Llywelyn family history. Morgan was asked if she would write an article for *Classic Magazine* about preparing for a place in the Olympics Dressage Team. When published it was accidentally noticed by Ruth Hatgood then the Chief Editor of a large publishing house who was interested in Dressage. The quality of Morgan's writing in this one article started her career as a writer producing her first book '*Wind from Hastings*'. The family moved to a large house in New Hampshire. Just as she had published her second book '*Lion of Ireland*' which went to the top in the bestsellers table, her husband Charlie passed away in 1984, so she packed up and moved to Ireland. She had to leave Atticus on veterinary advice with Lida Zang who was on the 1980 Olympic Team with her horse Fellow Traveller that was not allowed to compete in Moscow, as he had developed colon cancer. When Atticus finally passed away Linda sent Morgan his forelock that she still treasures to this day.

Morgan considered Atticus irreplaceable, so she concentrated on writing, and in 26 years she has written 20 novels and numerous short stories. Books such as *Brian Boro Emperor of the Irish, Finn Mac Cool, Strongbow, Druids, The Last Prince of Ireland, The Horse Goddess*. She has released four books to date in her Irish History Series such as *1916, 1921, 1949* and *1972*. Next year she will publish her next book *1999* which will complete the century and the series. She has won numerous International awards including the 1999 Exceptional Celtic Woman of the Year. She is a founding member of the Irish Writers Centre and former Chairman of the Irish Writers Union. She has walked the 427 miles from Malin Head to Mizen Head to support her favourite charities. When President Ronald Reagan was in the White House he often used extracts from Morgan's books in his speeches, which resulted in an open door in Washington for Charlie and herself.

Looking Back

Morgan still loves horses, but does not ride anymore, as her focus is now on writing, and because of her worldwide success with over 70 million copies of her work sold to date, she is under contract which sees most of her time decided by her publishing house. There have been many outstanding occasions in her life, but she sometimes reflects on the day of the final trial of her dressage test at Gladstone Park on her talented horse Atticus, that saw them relegated by the smallest of margins to reserve instead of being on the medal winning American Olympic Dressage Team that competed in Montreal in 1976. As a person that has been successful in many fields her advice is, 'Turn your time to things that you can succeed at', which is good advice from one who knows.

Jack Lambert

No sooner has one hunting season finished, when Jack Lambert is counting the days to the next hunting season such is his passion for the sport. He wears his age of more than three score and ten lightly, and nothing gives him more pleasure than riding his pure Irish Draught colt across the double banks of his native County Wexford.

He is a brave horseman who has also excelled as a point to point rider. A dedicated breeder of the native breed of Irish Draught horse, he stands his stallion Grange Bouncer who passes on his kind nature to his progeny. The stallion is a Grade A showjumper and an International Three Day Eventer. Jack is not one to keep his stallions in cotton wool, and insists that they get out hunting with the Killinick Harriers every week, as he maintains that it keeps them fresh, and they develop that balance and reliability that the Irish Draught horse is renowned for.

When I was reporting on the Killinick Harriers Hunt at Killinick village a couple of years ago I met Jack Lambert for the first time. He asked me if I had my camera ready, and I photographed him jumping a four foot hedge with a similar number of strands of barbed wire, and a drop of a few more feet on the other side. A normal enough hunting fence you might say, but the remarkable thing about it was that he was riding a 3 year old colt, and their combined ages came to 75 years of age. Jack is a legendary horseman and stallion master around Killinick in Co Wexford. Hunting is his passion in life, and he is counting the days to next season. But Jack would also be well known for the Irish Draught Grade A Showjumper and Open Eventing stallion Grange Bouncer by Prospect Pride (Registered Irish Draught 738), that he stands on his farm at Ashfield outside Wexford town. Both the stallion and her dam Grange Heather (RID 10331) are home bred. Now a 13 year old, he has been hunting since he was a three year old. Besides getting regular numbers of half-breds and Irish Draughts, he is also getting a lot of well-bred thoroughbreds, like the morning of my visit he had already covered an Old Vic and an Oscar mare, and he is as expected full for this season. As well as having a busy stud season, the stallion hunts all during the Winter, and he is so placid and has such a super temperament that many young people have had their first hunt on him. In fact he carried five different young people out on their first day's hunting last season, and I had the pleasure of hunting him myself at a meet at The Dirr, and he was a perfect gentleman, taking his turn when asked and showing terrific scope over the double banks and drains. Reflecting on the stallion's first day hunting, Jack recalls jumping 9 narrow double banks in succession, and he calculated that he had him fully broken to hunting by the fifth bank, as the stallion had mastered them so well. He had just started another eventing season competing at Willie Leahy's Dartfield track, finishing runner up in the CCIJ* ridden by Monica Whelan. Jack's regular hunter is the colt Killinick Rebel. He also has a nice 2 year old colt by Crosstown Dancer out of a Celtic Gold mare, that will be his next stallion. Two of Jack's daughters have followed him into horses, Claire who is a very accomplished event rider is now campaigning on John Keane's team of eventers. One of the high points of 2006 for Claire as a rider was the winning of the 4 Year Old Young Eventer Class at the Royal Dublin Society Show on All the Aces. The horse was bought by Jack at Goresbridge Sales and passed onto Claire who sold him in turn to John Keane. On being complimented on her magnificent win after her lap of honour in the Main Arena, she modestly replied that, "It is easy to win on a good one". His other daughter Ann is full time training point to pointers at home, and getting winners on the track, particularly with her good horse Shuil Coillte.

Point to Pointing

From an early age Jack has been riding ponies and horses on the family farm. Being sent to St. Peters in Wexford boarding school was not Jack's idea of how to spend the hunting season, so he was relieved to get it over with so he could get back to the horses full time. He has a charmed life hunting with the Killinicks and the Brees, with of course occasional days out with the Island and the Wexford Foxhounds as well. When he was younger he combined hunting with point to pointing, and one of his best pointers was Marley Lace by Interlace, and he takes great delight in recounting the story of one of his wins over the natural banks. The horse was so fresh after winning the first race of the Killinick Point to Point that he ran him again in the last race and won that also. He had planned to put £7 on her to win both races, but he lost it playing poker the previous Sunday, so not alone had he to borrow the entry fee of 10 shillings and £1 for the jockeys valet from his father, but he had to go and borrow again from him to celebrate the success in the Talbot Hotel in Wexford that night. His father was obviously a very understanding man! Another horse that won four races for him was Stickeyback, so named as it was his fathers favourite song. The horse was bought from Ned Cash who he always found easy to deal with. He won two divisions of the mare's race in Dungarvin in one afternoon, but before he could sell her, she broke down. Racing was all fun to Jack, particularly when he recalls with a smile the day his friend Benny Walsh fell at the first bank in a race, and when asked what type of horse he was riding, he replied "A right lepper"!

Hunting and Hunting Friends

Jacks two hunting pals of incidentally similar ages are former point to point riders, James O'Connor and Mick Berry. Mick of course is a brother of Padge, and will be remembered for riding winners such as Sandy Bow who won seven point to points, and Sir Daniel and Gypsy King. James has produced, ridden, and trained horses such as Killinick King, Killinick Buck, Love and Porter and Cloney Grange who won the Ladbrokes, and was considered very unlucky in Aintree, when going well before falling the second time around at Beechers. Another good horse was Quick Trip that won the Munster National ridden by David O'Connor. He is the father of jockeys Warren and 'Doc' O'Connor, the latter who is retired from riding and is training at home.

The trio reckon that they have the best three hunting horses in the country, Jack on his colt Killinick Rebel, Mick on his black horse Spitfire and James on Jacko a five year old, that he maintains jokingly that his dam's name was Careless! He bought him from the late Mrs. Leonard of Carne. Furthermore they find that the same horses carry them all season, which they put down to the Irish Draught blood, as they say the only injury that will stop the Irish Draught is a bad cut. A Wexford hunt horse has to be able to think, as it is asked many serious questions in the course of a hunt. They have to learn not alone to jump a wide ditch to the top of a steep bank, but often to steady and slide down the other side until they can get their footing for a good take off to jump the ditch on the other side. If they rush it they will pay the penalty. Jack remembers days when they could jump as many as 40 banks before they would get a run, as they are always crossing country, and stay away from the roads. Although full of praise for the sport with the current Killinicks master and huntsman John Stafford, Jack remembers great hunts with the late Jack Deacon, who he regarded as being an exceptional horseman, during the four seasons that he acted as huntsman. Also with Matt Roche when he hunted both the Bree and the Killinicks. Jack and James whipped in briefly, but they admit that they tended to loose the run of themselves, and often left the hounds behind as they were more interested in riding on at the challenging bank country. He recalls hunting one day with Michael Ryan son of Scarteen master Thady, and coming to a line of five barbed wire fences about four feet high, in succession by the side of a river. Michael asked Jack for his hunting jacket to put on the wire. But Jack having more respect for his good jacket, instead asked Michael for his crop and just drove on and took them like a showjumper. As Jack says "Needs must". Another day he tried an unbroken cob over a five bar gate at a nearby hunt; some of the followers were so impressed that Jack told them that with that kind of ability that he would take the cob home and break him properly! In order to keep going they each have had to acquire a few spare parts, Jack has a plate and pins in his leg as a result of an injury, and James has an excellent X-ray which he keeps convenient to show friends of the metal that was inserted last year in his broken ankle, both of which cause great fun when they are going through the metal detectors in security when going on their annual hunting holiday in America. Mick not to be outdone is deliberating on whether he will get his hip operated on before the hunting season begins. They each profess to be hard of hearing, which they find very convenient when the field master calls them back, obviously to no avail.

With 150 seasons of hunting with the Killinicks between them, and combined ages of over 200 years, they don't lack experience. The attraction of hunting for them in this rural area is the excitement and the danger of crossing natural bank country, as well as the fun when meeting all their hunting friends again after the Summer. The routine will be the same as previous seasons, hunt all Winter with the Killinicks, the Bree and the odd day with the Wexford and the Island, and then up to the Ward Union Staghounds where they have a reciprocal arrangement with Joint Master Sean Byrne who arranges horses for them as they do when the Ward members visit Killinick. They end the season with their friends in the Genesee Valley Hunt in New York. What an ideal life.

Charlie O'Neill

Charlie O'Neill has achieved many of his life's ambitions, particularly earning a living from his equestrian centre and hunter hirelings, which gives him an excuse to go hunting himself four or five times a week. He has owned some good race horses like Abbeylands that he rode over the banks course at the Punchestown Racing Festival, and he has also gone clear around Cheltenham.

A personal friend of Rolling Stones band member Ron Wood, he says he is the only person to play the spoons with members of the group!. He has also swapped hunting and racing stories with Prince Charles while on a sailing holiday in the Isles of Scilly. More recently in addition to his normal fund raising campaigns for charities, he has received support from his many friends for his fund raising trip riding a Harley Davidson motorbike to Alaska to support Beaumont Hospital in Dublin.

They say a picture paints a thousand words, and it was never so true as when I walked around the horse barn of that well known equestrian Charlie O'Neill at his home at Abbeyfields outside Clane in County Kildare. The walls were literally a who's who of society, Prince Charles having a smile for the camera in deep conversation with his namesake Charlie holding a glass of the best Irish whiskey in his hand, Ron Wood, Charlie Watts and Keith Richards of the Rolling Stones, Amber Dickle the previous owner of Aintree Grand National winner Amberleigh House, various Government Ministers like Mary Harney, and Tom Parlon, and a lovely home made card suitably inscribed 'Charlie you are a Star, Love Gilli and Sue'! Other photos in the gallery are of Charlie race riding in Punchestown and Cheltenham, and as Master of the Kildare Foxhounds and with the followers of the North Kildare Farmers, all with smiles on their faces. Why because it is fun to be with Charlie O'Neill, his customers like him, he looks after them, and they keep coming back, and introducing more of their friends to him.

You will always hear Charlie before you see him, as he seems to be permanently happy especially when he is sitting on a horse. He loves the species, horses are Ireland to him, reared on the family farm at Abbeylands, he had his first hunt on a white pony named Blossom with the Naas Harriers, and had great fun competing in all the local gymkhanas. Keen to imitate the jockeys he rode very short and was being constantly warned by Pam O'Mahony to let them down a hole or two but he would not listen. Joining the Kildare Pony Club under District Commissioners Bridget O'Brien-Butler and the Baroness de Robeck, the highlight of the year was Pony Camp on Punchestown Racecourse, when at that time the children would sleep in the racecourse buildings. The real hunting fun started when his father, who had bouts of illness that necessitated Charlie leaving school at 15 years of age, bought him a liver chestnut docktailed cob, which kept Charlie at the front of the Kildare Foxhounds, and the Naas Harriers. Desmond Guinness and Lord Patrick Conolly Carew were amongst his contemporaries at the time. About this time they changed from mixed farming to dairying with up to 120 cows to milk morning and evening, a schedule that had to fit into the hunting routine. In 1961 Peter McCreery Senior bought the farm next to them, and Charlie offered him the use of his fields to gallop his horses while he was undertaking building stables for his horses in training. It was very opportune as it also provided Charlie with an opportunity to fulfill his ambition of riding and handling race horses. He rode out two lots every morning which helped prepare him for race riding. He loved the buzz of the jockey room and the speed of racing. The whole country seemed to have come across his good hunter Abbeylands by Dreamy Eyes, that was distinctive for the small lump he had on his belly, a horse he bought for £70 as a yearling in the Bog of Allen and got £5 luck money. At the time he had no horse trailer, so he borrowed an open cattle trailer to bring him home. The horse hunted, hunter trialled, teamchased and even ran in the famous La Touche banks race at the Punchestown Racing Festival. Charlie and Abbeylands got around safely and received a hollor from the crowd as he passed the finish at the stands, and of course standing up in his stirrups he hollored back. He was a special horse that Charlie kept for himself, although he thinks that he may have loaned him for a hunt to showjumper Tommy Brennan at one time. On another occasion he was riding the mare Cutty Sark owned by Mrs. Guy Shorrocks in a hurdle race at Naas. Coming around the last bend Pat Taaffe called to Charlie to move out to give him a clear run on the rails. Charlie was taken aback for a moment as he was flattered that one of his heroes Pat Taaffe would know his name. He had great fun riding his own horse Hellfire Hostess coming second in the Fairyhouse Hurdle, followed by winning a bumper and a hurdle race at Navan. But Cheltenham was where he always wanted to ride, and he aimed her at the Sun Alliance Hurdle in 1978. The weather was a mixture of heavy rain and high winds, and both Charlie and Peter McCreery stood at the jockey room door wondering whether they would race or not. The situation was not made any easier when a light aircraft crashed in the high winds into the course rails. However his luck was in, racing was on, and he got around, coming a very respectable 10th of 28 runners. They came home that night as he had 120 cows to milk the following morning.

The 1970's saw Charlie getting seriously into hunting and cross country horses with the patronage of Dublin businessmen Pierre Doyle, Kenny White, Maurice Cully and others. He boarded their horses and transported them to all the popular packs in Leinster. The recession in the 1980's and high double digit interest rates changed his business again, as most people did not want to board horses, but wanted to hire them when they needed them, so Charlie bought a supply of horses that kept his customers and visitors well supplied. He was so hunting mad that at one time he hunted 11 consecutive days, with four different packs. In 1985 he got out of dairying and changed to suckler calves, which was a much easier operation. They sold their farm Abbeylands later in 1999 for development. He and his wife Mary and family transferred their operation to Abbeyfields a 250 acre farm down the road that his father had bought in 1934 for £1400, which his neighbours thought was a very high price to pay at the time! He is self sufficient and grows his own haylage, corn and straw. With a green field site he built 50 stables with all the ancillary facilities, which has turned out to be one of the most modern equine enterprises in the country. And instead of relying on only hunt hirelings which was previously an October to March business, it is now an all year around business, offering livery, hirelings, and a cross country course as well as full, half and group livery. He also provides all the sporting requirements for hotels and country clubs like the K Club, the Four Seasons, Luttrellstown and others in the area with Clay Pigeon Shooting, Archery and Quad riding. He feels that he is very fortunate that his son Daragh who hunted, point to pointed and studied at Warrenstown Agricultural College together with his wife Grainne came into the business full time with him. Having similar personalities, they run an open house for all the customers providing a very homely and personal service. He was invited to be joint master of the Kildare

Foxhounds a position he held for 10 years. As a number of his clients wanted to go cross country riding on a Sunday, he set up the North Kildare Farmers, which sees up to 100 followers on any given weekend enjoying a spin over natural country without hounds, combined with supporting many charitable causes in the area with the proceeds. Donations managed by their Secretary/Treasurer Pat Murphy have been made to village schools, Riding for the Disabled, Kildare Hospice, ICA, Gaelic Football Clubs, village tidy town groups and Marian Finucane's AIDS Program. Rolling Stone friend Ron Wood who is an accomplished artist donates a painting every year for the Charity Auction.

He still loves to go racing and got a great kick out of the Martin Pipe trained Ilnamar by Official owned by his friend Joe Moran win in the Coral Cup in Cheltenham in 2002. Charlie was in such good voice hugging the trainer's wife that many people thought that he was the owner, especially when the crowd were shouting "Well done Charlie".

To get away from the daily grind of the business Charlie goes skiing, or takes to the road on his Harley Davidson motorbike. Again he confesses that when he bought it from a man in Carlow he had to take it home in a trailer packed with tyres to protect it travelling as he did not know how to ride it. But like everything else in Charlie O'Neill's life, when he takes something up he masters it. A few years ago he and his pals rode down to Morocco on their Harley Davidson motorbikes, and followed that by a trip to St Tropez in the South of France. His favourite saying is 'It's nice to be nice' and 'When you'r good you'r good'. In fact his latest fund raising project was riding a Harley Davidison to Alaska for Beaumont Hospital in Dublin. Life has been good to Charlie O'Neill, the only man to play the spoons with the Rolling Stones when they were attempting a piece of Irish traditional music at a party, and his chance meeting with Prince Charles when a local policeman in Saint Mary's in the Isles of Scilly thought he was part of the World Press when he showed him his tiny instamatic box camera as proof that he was a photographer! As he says "I have been a very lucky man, to be able to make a living out of what I love best, and fortunate to have such a nice family".

Captain John Wentges

In 1952 Captain John Wentges arrived in Dublin as part of the Dutch Showjumping Team competing at the Royal Dublin Society Annual Show. He was so taken with Ireland that he decided to stay.

He married Rosemary Woods of Milverton Hall, and enjoyed himself so much hunting that he retired from showjumping. He became joint master of the Fingal Harriers Hunt and also formed his own pack the Little Grange Harriers. For 45 seasons he followed the Ward Union Staghounds, taking responsibility for hound breeding when they hunted a pack of pure Dumfriesshire hounds.

When competing in the Monte Carlo Car Rally he was the only competitor to wear a bowler hat for the duration of the event.

Captain John Wentges came to Ireland in 1952 as part of the Dutch Showjumping Team who were competing at the Royal Dublin Society, and ironically enough that was the last time he showjumped, remaining a dedicated hunting man ever since, serving as master and huntsman of a number of packs in the meantime. Although he drag hunted on horseback with hounds following an artificial scent in Holland, the freedom of natural hunting in Ireland allowed him to pursue his wider passion for the sport, and his lifelong interest in hounds. He met and married the late Rosemary Woods of Milverton Hall a keen hunting lady, and they were popular figures following the Ward Union Staghounds, the Meaths, Louths and the Fingal Harriers. The Wentges home of Milverton Hall Estate is just on the outskirts of the seaside town of Skerries in North County Dublin, but it is probably better known as the popular venue for the Ward Union Annual Hunter Trials for the last 25 years, with its Tommy Brennan designed course, but it has other strong connections with hunting, carriage driving, hunter trials and eventing.

The hunting tradition of the Woods family started back in 1849 when the Honorable George Woods kept his own pack of hounds known as Mr. Woods Hounds at Milverton Hall and hunted fox. When the Fingal Harriers were founded later in 1881 his relation Richard (Dickie) Woods of Whitestown House, the Naul, took over the mastership which was to last for another 20 seasons.

Hunting and Hounds

But the family association with hunting was not to end there. Captain Wentges, by now enjoying his association with the neighbouring packs of the Fingal Harriers, the Ward Union Staghounds and the Louth Foxhounds decided that he did not like the long breaks between hunting seasons, so he decided to form his own Otterhound Pack, which he named the Blackwater Otter Hounds, and hunted the rivers around Drogheda and the Boyne during the Summer. He was later invited to become joint master of the Fingals with the late Denis Mahony better known as a founding member of Keane Mahony Smith the auctioneering company and father of Edmund Mahony, master of the Louth Foxhounds and Chairman of Tattersalls whose family have close connections with the Galway Blazers. After spending a number of seasons with the Fingals he was approached by Barbara Jennings of the Little Grange Harriers to take over the hunting of the pack which he agreed to, and kennelled them in Milverton Hall in the kennels that were used originally for Mr. Woods Hounds. He and his followers enjoyed many years hunting up as far as the River Boyne, often hosting joint meets with George Briscoe the master of the Tara Harriers. During this time he was a regular follower of the Ward Union Staghounds, hunting first with them in 1954 which was to last 45 seasons when he retired from hunting. His lifelong interest in hounds got him very involved in the breeding of the Ward Staghounds, and as he had a great friendship with Sir Rupert Buchanan-Jardine, Master of the Dumfriesshire Hounds, he introduced an outcross of the Dumfriesshire into the Ward Union Staghounds breeding programme. It was fantastic to see these unique black long legged foxhounds pursue the deer with their deep bellowing voices that could be heard for miles around. His expert knowledge of the Dumfriesshire hound has led him to write a detailed history of the breed, which now extends to three volumes, complete with records of breeding, tracing back the foundation hounds to France. Being such enthusiastic supporters of hunting in the North County both Captain

Wentges and his wife Rosemary were made honorary life members of both the Wards Union Staghounds and the Fingal Harriers.

Horses

Although he was mainly associated with showjumping in Holland, in Ireland he enjoyed going to horse fairs to buy suitable hunting horses that could be ridden also by all his family. One such instance was when he bought what he regards as his best horse Sovereign almost palomino in colour at Cahermee Fair in Cork. He had forgotten to bring his cheque book, but the owner Mr. O'Driscoll from the Carberry Hounds knew that he was a paid up master of harriers so they agreed to create their own temporary cheque until funds were transferred on his return, an example at a time when a gentleman's word was his bond. The horse proved to be the ideal all rounder, hunting hounds all during the season, and winning the Boland Carriage Driving Cup twice. As the Captain and his family were very tall in stature he had a tendency to buy very large horses, so he had to raise the roof of his horsebox, so it was known jokingly as the giraffe box.

Family

Another favourite horse was Oliver bought from the well known horse breeder John Stewart, which his talented daughter Fiona campaigned to considerable success in eventing, winning a European Silver Medal in Punchestown. The Captain determined that Fiona would own a good horse, sold Oliver to her for one shilling, an extremely generous exchange. She later went on to compete with him in many of the top events in England including Badminton. Fiona studied under Jackie Doherty for her AI at Ashton Equestrian Center, and evented two of Jackie's horses, Brimstone and Argyle at Wylie. One of the proudest moments came when Fiona was selected for the Irish Team to compete at the Los Angeles Olympics, riding the flying grey Ballylusky.

The Captain was a familiar sight at the Los Angeles Olympics, testing security, going from one compound to another carrying just a plastic bucket and sponge, and at no time was he stopped by security. The family talents were not to stop there, as Libby his daughter-in-law produced a number of winners from her good mare Suffer in Silence by Red Regent, particularly Caerphilly by Welsh Term who won the Small Riding Horse Championship in Dublin ridden by Jane Bradbury. This was followed by two more of her progeny Victorious Day by Glenagyle Rebel runner up in the Small Hunter Class in Dublin ridden by Mairead Ryan, and another runner up Beethoven by Crosstown Dancer ridden by Mairead's husband Kieran.

Captain Wentges' son Richard, an architect by profession, is the artist in the family like his mother Rosemary, and many will have seen his fine watercolors reproduced in *The Irish Field* of the fences that Tommy Brennan designed for the European Championships in Punchestown a few years ago.

His other son Michael who hunted and hunter trialled as a child, but whose main pastime is shooting, has represented Ireland in Match Rifle Shooting competitions both at home and abroad on a number of occasions, while also managing the family's considerable estate giving invaluable support as host to hunting, eventing and hunter trials. He and his wife Libby's daughters Sophie, Rosemary and Hannah continue the hunting tradition getting out regularly with the local packs, as well as being active members of Meath Pony Club where their grandmother Rosemary was District Commissioner.

Little did Captain Wentges know when he came to Ireland as a member of the Dutch Showjumping Team in 1952 that he would live such a fulfilled life of fun with his family in North County Dublin, serving as master of three packs of hounds, as well as enjoying hunting with so many other packs, while pursuing his hobby of carriage driving and breeding hounds. But then he had a reputation of doing things with style, particularly when the year before he came to Ireland, he is on record as having driven a Volkswagen Beetle car in the famous Monte Carlo Rally wearing his bowler hat all the way, even in the mountain stages! But most of all he had the pleasure of seeing his daughter Fiona achieve the highest honor in equestrian sport of representing her country in eventing at the Los Angeles Olympic Games. With three International representatives in one family, in three different sports, now that's an achievement worth noting.

Captain John Wentges with the Fingal Harriers

Bill Bourns

Bill Bourns has one of the most successful records of producing show cobs in Ireland. With an interest in cooking and entertaining, most of her horses have culinary names like, Piece Of Cake, Oysters For Dinner and Time For A Gin. One of the horses that she was associated with, Tom Firr won the Championship at the Horse Of The Year Show in England.

Her talents do not rest there, as she was also a point to point rider, a thoroughbred breeder, and an enthusiastic hunt follower of both the East Galway Foxhounds and the Galway Blazer Foxhounds.

Just glancing at the names of the large number of show horses produced by Bill Bourns immediately conjures up a connection with cooking and entertainment. Names like Time for a Gin, Oysters for Dinner and Piece of Cake, names that really have meaning in her life and of course there is a connection to her interests, but more of that later.

Bill's first name is misleading, as for those that know her, they know Bill Bourns is a lady. She blames her sister Shirley who could not pronounce her real name as a child, but she also admits that her parents were expecting a boy, so she was not too put out. And there is no point confusing things further by telling you what her real first name is, but I am sure that you are by now curious!

Family Background
Bill, aside from her interest in the wider circle of equestrian sports, has been a frequent winner showing horses in the ring for many years now. But where

does all this interest in horses come from? Her family were substantial farmers in East Galway, and she admits that the main influence on her was that of her mother Mavis who was from Nenagh in Tipperary. From a point to pointing family, her mother hunted with the Nenagh Harriers and when she settled in East Galway she hunted with the local foxhounds when Paddy Pickersgill and Lancelot Smith were hunting hounds. Her mother had an interest in buying and selling horses and ponies, so all her children including Bill and Shirley who is now joint master of the Galway Blazers, and their brother Richard were all mounted on good ponies. His son Andrew is well known in showjumping having represented his country on numerous occasions but has now moved into horses. Shirley's daughter Sorcha has been very successful showing and eventing Lady Hemphill's pony Tulira Katie Daly, and she is now also competing on horses. Things were not always as buoyant as at the moment, as there was literally no leisure market for horses at the time. Her father Tommy hunted a little when he was a child, but although his interest was in mainstream farming he was very supportive of his family's involvement in equine activities. Even when Bill was at Rathdown School then in Monkstown County Dublin, she managed to spend some time each week at Dudgeon's at Burton Hall Equestrian Center. One of her best ponies was a Connemara called Flicka she hunted with the Easy Galways that was later sold to France.

The inspiration in naming her horses is connected to the time she studied hotel management in Cathal Brugha Street College in Dublin. Cooking was and still is one of her great passions in life. She is an excellent cook and hostess. Another one of her interests are pigs, and she is the proud owner of a Vietnamese pot belly pig. Not surprisingly many of the ornaments in her kitchen have images of pigs, and even the weather vane on her house has the silhouette of a pig on it. Her favorite dish besides desserts is not pork understandably, but roast beef remaining loyal to beef farmers in East Galway like her brother Andrew.

Back to Horses in Galway

Although she worked in the catering industry for some time she was always drawn back to Galway and hunting. But she was also drawn to point to pointing, and her first break literally in more ways than one came when she rode Jimmy Coulihan's Tinkers Deal in the East Galway Members Race, unfortunately ending in hospital with a broken collar bone. But not being put off by a minor problem she came back the year after and won it on the same horse. Michael Dempsey joint master of the Galway Blazers Foxhounds recognised that she needed a schoolmaster horse to let her get some enjoyment, and particularly gain more experience of race riding, so he organised a loan of an experienced mare called Mini Bus, so named as you could not push her too much when exercising her on the roads! This mare gave her the experience to advance in her race riding. Her first racehorse was The Wee Major bred by Michael Dempsey, who she broke and got him hunting before going on to race. Although Bill usually rode him, the first day he won she gave the ride to her cousin Peter McCutcheon. He was later sold on to Paul Green. Bill had a very simple approach, although she loved the thrill of speed over the fences, if one of her horses had a real chance she would always put a better rider up. Another of her winners was Some Tulip that won the Blazers Members Race, and Some Daisy, a filly who won a number of point to points that trainer of the champion chaser Best Mate Tom Costello later purchased. One of her most difficult horses to break was Sam Shorrock by Vividari, but she persevered and got the measure of him and pointed him successfully, winning four times before selling him to Graham Thorner in England where he later won a number of hunter chases. Ivy Blue was another winner, but she kept her as a brood mare. She considers Fidel Express as her best. She went to Tattersals to buy a store horse, and for some reason liked the look of him. Her mother was with her and she thought that she was mad, as she always liked to break the horses herself, and this fellow was 4 year old and already broken. But her instinct told her that there was something about him she liked. She started hunting and schooling him, and he won two point to points with Pat Bohan up. He was later bought by Tom Costello and sold on to Arthur Stephenson in England. Rough Justice was another that she produced and sold on to Tony Mullins. She still keeps a few thoroughbred brood mares and has some progeny by Cashel Court that was with the trainer Michael Cunningham before she stood him on her farm. She also has brood mares by Aristocracy, including a smart Moscow Society colt and another by Eves Error. She has had stallions standing at farm, particularly Corridini and War Hero.

Show Cobs

Having been mainly associated with thoroughbreds she initially looked on cobs as non athletic and not very handsome. But that changed when she bought her first cob Flashy, which she did not show as her neighbor Susan Stoney thought that he was such a good model that she bought him. Bill got to like riding them and got hooked when she started to win at provincial shows. A cob according to Bill is a miniature heavyweight hunter, but she insists on quality, otherwise they will not move or ride well. She likes a good hard color like dark brown or bay, but admits that greys are popular with English buyers and colored cobs are now getting popular. She sources her young stock from the various fairs like Ballinasloe and Spancil Hill, and because she is so well known as a cob producer people just contact her if they have something nice. It is now 25 years ago since she started showing ponies, thoroughbreds and now mainly cobs at the Royal Dublin Society Annual Show. She admits that it is always a lucky show for her, both in winning and also as important in selling. An interesting observation which says it all is, that she maintains that it is easier to buy a cob from a person that does not know that they have one! There have been so many good cobs that she has produced over the years that she just rhymes them off randomly. Cute Suit was sold to England and is doing well. Just a Chance a Reserve Champion in the RDS (Royal Dublin Society) is now hunting with the Andrews Bridge Hunt in America. Heres Harry won for two years at RDS, is now in England and Tommy Tully who has won twice at the RDS and was Champion in 1997, well Bill not only sold him but bought him back, and then resold him again, making a better profit the second time around. Just to prove a point, she also added a Small Hunter Championship in the RDS with Oysters For Dinner which she bred herself. Time For A Gin was second twice in the RDS has been sold to a client in England where he has been winning regularly, under his new name Macmillan. Piece Of Cake who was second in the RDS and is also competing in England. Minor Detail another of her cobs is now in the working hunter class, and Man With A Plan who was fourth in the RDS, has since been sold on to a customer in Texas. A nice cob that she sold to Donald Mills in Wexford was Ikey Bell, that she feels has a good future, and deep down she would like to have held onto him. Her most successful cob bought at Ballinasloe Fair was Tom Firr, who won the Championship at the Horse of the Year Show in England. Philip Scott, himself a very successful producer has ridden the cob in most of the horse's competition outings.

She has four cobs to campaign this year as well as other young stock. A four year old colored heavyweight that she bought in Spancil Hill, and two greys, a five and six year old that are backed and riding, and a dark brown five year old. She has a similar routine each year in preparing them. After some hunting she lets them down for about 6 weeks, but they are kept shod and fed beet pulp nuts, oats and boiled barley. She admits to being a traditionalist when it comes to feeding, plenty of grain as she was brought up at a time when oats was the main hard feed. They are then taken in at the end of March and are wormed and have their teeth done. The ground work then begins, building up slowly with plenty of roadwork and hacks through the woods. By the end of May they start showing on the Western circuit, moving on to Mullingar, Longford and other shows. This is to give them plenty of exposure to the public, and be in the company of other horses. Although some of her customers come to her around this time, she likes to give her cobs a chance in Dublin, but if she is made an offer she cannot refuse, then that is a different matter. Of course she is already looking for young stock for the year ahead, and she always has a number bought well in advance so that she can do some early work with them.

What are her ambitions for the future? Well the first one is never to retire, and the second is to go on buying, showing and selling show cobs, and trying to get the very best of their potential out of them in the showring. And in her own words, "Roll on the Royal Dublin Society Show next year", and expect to read about some more culinary named winners.

Sheila Mullins on the Lassie Film Set

Chantal Deon

Chantal Deon whose family name is d'Arc, the same family name as the French heroine that we know as Joan of Arc, spent her childhood riding French Cavalry horses as her father was a French Army General and later Commander in Chief.

Since setting up home in Ireland over 30 years ago, she was invited to become a joint master of the East Galway Foxhounds, a position she has held since 1988.

But she is also well known as one of the most successful breeders of the native Irish Draught horse, and one of her mares won 122 times in 9 years, which included 11 Championships.

One of the most successful show breeders of the native Irish Draught Horse is Chantal Deon, from the Old Rectory Stud, Tynagh in County Galway. Her diminutive figure is a familiar sight leading her brood mares and their foals around all the major show rings of Ireland.

Childhood in France
Before settling in Ireland Chantal led a very interesting and varied life in her home country of France, as well as living in different parts of the world, very seldom being far away from horses. Her father Renaudeau d'Arc was a General in the French Army, eventually becoming Commander in Chief. The family name certainly is a head turner especially in France, as it is the family name of the French heroine that we know as Joan of Arc. Chantal was born in Paris but like many French families, they also had a holiday home in

Normandy where they spent their Summers. Her grandfather was master of a wild boar pack in Normandy, and owned a number of race horses, while her mother's father was a keen amateur jockey, and rode in the Grand Steeple-Chase de Paris that is run annually on Auteuil Racecourse, known as le Temple de l'Obstacle in the Bois de Boulogne close to Longchamp Racecourse. Unusually Chantal never began riding on ponies as other children did, as from a very young age she always had a stable of French Army Cavalry horses to choose from. She mainly showjumped, competing in Rabat in Morocco as well as Estoril in Portugal and in the Spetsai Islands in Greece, just three of the other countries that she lived in. Fortunately there were lots of ladies competitions in these countries and she was quite successful in the National competitions. She stopped riding for 7 years after she married her husband, the well known French novelist Michael Deon, author of books such as The Purple Taxi, Wild Ponies and The Wild Geese, a number of which were later made into films. Chantal was busy typing while her husband did the writing. He was honoured nationally in 1975 with the distinction of the Prix du Achadamie, of which there are only 45 members.

Moving to Ireland

During this time her son Alexander and daughter Alice were born, and they started dividing their time between Greece and Ireland. Initially they stayed at Kilcolgan Castle in County Galway and this was followed by brief spells at Lough Cutra Castle outside Gort, and St Clerans in Craughwell the former home of film director John Huston. Keen to get back to the horses Chantal visited Chris and Eugene Daly's stables at Raheen in Athenry. They used to supply most of the hirelings to the Blazers at the time, and although they were suggesting that she should hunt, she started riding out instead. But she was soon to join them, as everybody seemed to be off hunting in the Winter. Chantal bought a mare from Willie Leahy which she hunted and used to enjoy hacking his horses to and from meets, while her children hunted Willie's ponies. Around this time Chantal bought the Old Rectory which is an old glebe house outside Tynagh in East Galway. From there she could finally set down roots and plan the accommodation for the horses that they planned to stable. As hunting was such a popular sport in the area, Chantal got so involved that she was appointed joint Master of the East Galway Foxhounds, a position that she has occupied since 1988.

Now that she had her own base to work from, one of her early successes was a horse that she bought from Willie Leahy called Seman. Chantal showjumped and showed him in Dublin, and sold him during the show to Jean Marc Nicolas, from where he ended up jumping internationally for France winning a Grand Prix in Paris, and was later sold on to Italy. Kevin

Moloney who is now retired from showjumping rode all her horses to considerable success in competition, such as Aillebird by Athenius that they showjumped to Grade A level, and their good mare Daffney by Middle Temple.

Breeding the Irish Draught Horse

Little did Chantal know how successful she would be when she bought the Irish Draught mare Brehan Lass II by Legaun Prince out of Brehan Lass, by Kilcolman as a 2 year old. It is hard to believe that the filly failed the Registered Irish Draught inspection, which is ironic as she and her stock went on later to take the highest honors in showing. This was to be Chantal's foundation mare, and would begin her lifelong association with the Irish Draught breed, competing, breeding and winning all over the country. Bred by Sarah Campbell in Limerick she was bought initially at the local mart by a neighbour and sold on to Chantal. The mare proved to be the ideal multipurpose horse starting her showing career in 1987, and hunting with all the local foxhound packs particularly the East Galways. Brehan Lass II reached Grade B in showjumping before she was put in foal to Pride of Toames, producing the filly foal Brehan Pride. Brehan Lass who was retired at 24 years of age had produced 16 foals, amongst them a number of well known showjumpers Bran Flake by Aristocracy, who has had considerable success in Portugal, the stallion Cradilo by Kildalton Gold, who won the American Performance Championship and the North American Irish Draught Championship in 1998. Another jumper on the American circuit is Hermine. She also produced Belline Tynagh Gold a Grade A who won the six and seven year old in 1998 at the Royal Dublin Society. Brehan Lass II has a remarkable record as a broodmare, breeding 16 foals, and in just 7 years showing won 66 first prizes including 22 championships, amongst them the Kerrygold at Millstreet, and also jumping for the last time in foal as a Grade B showjumper in Simmonscourt in Dublin. Her last foal was in 2004, a chestnut colt named Supermarket by the thoroughbred Market Square, before the mare passed away herself, leaving a remarkable breeding and showing legacy. Although that was a difficult act to follow, her daughter Brehan's Pride by Pride of Toames practically doubled that showing performance. In 9 years of showing she was in the ribbons 122 times, of which 99 were first prizes, which included 6 championships in 1994 and 5 championships in 1998 including the Millstreet Kerrygold and the Royal Dublin Society (RDS) in 1992. She won the National Irish Draught Championship in 1993, and reserve in the RDS Breeders Championship, and champion at Balmoral in 1997. Another good year was 1999 which produced 21 first places, and in 2000 10 first prizes. Her progeny has included 5 stallions of which Herrero by Kildalton Gold currently stands in Florida. As a foal he won 15 first prizes alone, and with his dam they shared the Breeders Championship Reserve at the RDS. In 2004 she was covered by Grosvenor Lad again.

Her filly Gurraun My Way by Grosvenor Lad won 15 firsts and 6 championships as a foal, followed by 10 firsts and winner of the Mare of the Future competition the following year 2002, and the National Irish Draught Show as a 4 year old. In her third year of showing she won 12 firsts including 2 class wins at the National Show in Ennis and Young Mare Class Winner at the RDS. Her first foal a chestnut colt Carrabawn View won every time out as a foal, including champion at Tullamore and Reserve at the RDS, before being sold onto America. Her second foal is a filly Carrabawn Way.

She currently has a mix of brood mares, half breds and stallions, but the real pride of place goes to the pure Irish Draught foundation stock, and the list of successes just goes on with every new crop.

Starting out when she was buying her foundation stock, Chantal demonstrated her expert judgment of bloodstock when she pitted her eye for quality against the inspectors who originally rejected her champion foundation mare Brehan Lass II, and proved they were very wrong. So you feel privileged when she shares her expert views on what she looks for in her horses. She is very definite in the characteristics that she looks for to produce quality. First of all she likes a horse with a nice head. To complement this she does not like a body too big, but with a nice shoulder, and above all they must walk like a thoroughbred. A mare has to have a flowing action, and move from the shoulder down rather than from the knee, and to show her paces she must be capable of having a fast balanced gallop.

As the young stock and the brood mares are prepared for the forthcoming showing season, the Old Rectory Stud in Tynagh is in full swing with plans to retain many of the honours that have won in previous years, all started by that remarkable Irish Draught mare Brehan Lass II and her astute owner Chantal Deon.

Lady Anne Hemphill

Lady Anne Hemphill was field master of the Galway Blazer Foxhounds for 15 seasons, and being an accomplished horsewoman she gave a good lead to the followers across the Galway stone walls.

She founded the Tulira Connemara Pony Stud at her home at Tulira Castle with foundation mares that she purchased from Film Director John Huston when he was master of the Galway Blazers. Her stallion Tulira Robuck has been a frequent winner in the showring, and his progeny has been sold on to clients in many countries around the world.

My early memories of Lady Anne Hemphill were as field master of the Galway Blazers Foxhounds. Of course hunting was in her blood as she was a descendent of a famous Blazers master of 33 seasons Burton Persse. She gave a terrific lead across the famous Galway stone walls. I had a friend visit when Michael Dempsey was hunting hounds at the Riflerange in Oranmore. As usual Dempsey was oblivious of the dark, and hunted hounds every day as if it was his last. He found a fox at dusk, and we literally could only see a few yards ahead of us. Lady Anne's horse did a somersault jumping onto a lane, and all we could see was a hand waving with words of encouragement coming from behind the wall, saying "Go on, go on, don't wait for me". And go on we went, and she caught up as soon as she and her horse found their feet. Today she is known as a top judge and a breeder of Connemara pony champions from her stud originally at Tulira Castle and now at Kiltulla, outside Athenry in County Galway.

Childhood

Lady Anne Hemphill, formerly Anne Ruttledge was born in India, where her father Robin was serving with the Indian Cavalry as Commander of the Governor's Bodyguard in Madras. He was a noted ornithologist and author, and was awarded the Peter Scott award from Trinity College. Her mother was Rose Burke of Ballydugan, outside Loughrea, a cousin of George St. John Burke who I remember as one of the oldest men to ride in the Aintree Grand National on his two horses Uncle Whiskers and Irish Coffee. Her first taste of hunting came in India with the Peshawar Hounds where her father was master and huntsman. Most of her hunting was done with the Ootacamund Hounds in the Ooty Valley, where they still hunt today. In 1937 as an 8 year old the family returned from India and settled in her mother's native Cloonee near Hollymount in County Mayo. She wanted a pony so John Daly's father Paddy of Lough Mask House found her a pony near Screebe that did everything from bringing home turf from the bog, to transporting seaweed which was used as fertiliser. Paddy Moran who worked on the farm brought the dark brown Connemara back to their farm, and she was immediately named Peggy.

Hunting in Ireland

It was not long before the pair started hunting with the North Mayo Harriers, then hunted by Percy Dickenson who had hunted with the legendary master of the Blazers, Major Bowes Daly. The meets were at places like Castlebar, North Shore, Lough Carra and Roundfort. On other days they would transport the pony and horses by train to Ballyglunan to hunt with the Blazers at meets like Castlehackett when Paddy Pickersgill was hunting the hounds. Her mother was a familiar sight in the hunting field riding side saddle. She went to school in Mount Anville in Dublin, but she never considered herself a good student as the only thing on her mind was hunting. Soon after leaving school she and her glamorous sister Veronica were working in London and enjoying the social circle of hunt balls, parties and hunting with the Heythrop and coming back for the Galway Races. She met her husband Lord Peter Patrick Hemphill while he was studying at Oxford and the relationship developed, and they were married in 1950 in St. James Church by the Abbott of Downside School. She fell in love with Tulira Castle outside Ardrahan, and asked her father-in-law if they could go to live in it. It had no electricity and needed a lot of work. It was from here that they raised a family of two daughters Mary-Anne, Angela and a son Charles, and founded her famous Tulira Connemara Pony Stud. She hunted regularly with the Limerick, Scarteen and Westmeaths as well as her home pack the Blazers. But as she says it was easy to be hunting up to six days a week with a cook in the kitchen and grooms in the stables. Peter Patrick became joint master of the Blazers, and Anne served as master for a short time with Major Philip Profumo who was hunting hounds while Michael Dempsey was whipping in. She also served as field master for 15 seasons. One of her best horses was Rockmount that she purchased from trainer Tom Costello.

Co Galway Hunt Pony Club

She founded the County Galway Pony Club in 1963 which was the first west of the Shannon. They were some of her happiest days which were to go on for 25 years. They wore the maroon and white colours of Galway. The children were fortunate to have the services of Anita King, Helen Dennison and Colonel Dick Lovett, who was a fine horseman having trained at the Weedon Equitation School in Leicestershire, and later served in the Indian Cavalry. He was a familiar figure following the Blazers and was always conspicuous because of his perfect seat regardless of what type of country he was crossing. The pony rallies were held at Tulira Castle and on the Galway Racecourse in Ballybrit, and the Hemphills sent out their horse truck to collect any ponies of children that did not have transport. John Huston's daughter Angelica and son Tony were active members riding their Connemara ponies, and assisted by their stud groom Paddy Lynch.

In 1967 they started competing in eventing and the Galway Branch won the championships in 1969, 1972 and 1973. They were also placed in Stoneleigh in the same years, and some of their members achieved International honours on the Irish Junior Eventing Team. Her daughter Angela was on the first team that Pam Gillispie took to Germany, followed by disappointment when she was picked to go to Burghley in England only for her pony to go lame. Current master of the Blazers Rose Dempsey and her cousins huntsman Tom and his brother Pat all achieved representative honours.

Founding the Tulira Connemara Pony Stud

Anne Hemphill was having dinner one night in St Clerans with the then owner, film director John Huston who was master of the Galway Blazers and his wife Toni, when she spotted two Connemara ponies under the trees outside the diningroom. On enquiring from her host if they were for sale, he confirmed that they were, as he was planning to breed thoroughbreds. She purchased both, and they turned out to be her foundation Connemara pony mares, Glen Nellie and Star of Fahy. Glen Nellie was covered by the stallion Tooreen Ross and produced a colt Tulira Mairtin who got injured as a two year old, but went on to become the studs famous stallion. He had $8^1/_2$ inches of bone and was never broken but kept for stud duties. The filly Tulira

Mavourneen became champion at one and two years, and champion performance pony at the RDS in 1980. Always on the look out for good stock Anne Hemphill used to go regularly to Connemara, and on one occasion she spotted two nice ponies in a field near Screebe, but she had to tour around to find the owners. One was Glencaugh Lady who was later to produce foals by Carna Bobby, Nimble Dick and the rest by Tulira Mairtin, never missing going in foal. She won the first Confined Connemara Jumping competition at Galway Show. The other pony was special too, Noreen Grey who was thought to be infertile but when she got to Tulira she bred 10 foals in 11 years, most notably Tulira Rocket and two successful stallions Tulira Nimble Dick who went to Germany and Tulira Cloonee who went to France.

It turned out to be a much larger operation than was first envisaged, with more than 50 ponies in the operation at one time, all prizewinners, with progeny exported to nine different countries, like Cregmore Colm who was champion in Australia, Napoleon was exported to Libya, and Tulira Bobby to Holland. There was disappointment however in 1983 when the family home Tulira Castle was sold, and the stud had to be disbanded necessitating a dispersal sale of 56 top Connemara ponies with impeccable breeding.

However in 1988 Anne Hemphill reestablished the Tulira Connemara Pony Stud when they moved to Kiltulla with her Champion stallion Tulira Robuck who is a half brother of Tulira Fionn Macool, by Earl of Castle Ffrench out of Tulira Heather by Carna Bobby. As a 3 year old Tulira Robuck was champion at Claremorris Show also winning the 3 and 4 year old colt class at Clifden, as well as Reserve Supreme Champion. During his spell with producers Robin Avery and Chris Patrick in Lancashire, he won 16 championships, three supreme and one - hand championships, as well as 14 mountain and moorland classes, ridden by Chris Patrick and Paula Holden. He qualified for the Horse of the Year Show and also won the Open Riding Class Olympia Qualifier and Championship, and narrowly missed out on the championship in Olympia. In 2002 he won the Supreme Championship at Oughterard Show. Some of his young progeny are owned by people like Best Mate's trainer Henrietta Knight and flat trainer Jim Bolger. Three of Lady Anne Hemphill's current mares Tulira Noreen, Tulira Marble Rose and Tulira Katie Daly go back to the two foundation mares. The latter can be seen regularly competing on the showjumping, showing and eventing circuit ridden by Sorcha North, and was Champion Connemara Performance Champion Show at Ballinasloe in 2003, the All Ireland Ridden Championship and Supreme Champion, as well as winning the Cannon Ball Cup for the All Ireland Final at Oughterard in 2003. There have been a long line of equine achievers from the Tulira Stud that deserve a more lengthy publication than can be achieved in this short overview, as each year the honours and achievements continue.

Current Interests

Today Lady Anne Hemphill can be seen at race meetings around the country as her husband Lord Peter Patrick Hemphill has been a senior steward of the Turf Club for many years. Pakie Whelan, her stud groom, continues to be part of the stud's success, and she still follows the Blazers but now by car, and is very much in demand as a judge of Connemera classes. A considerable amount of her time is spent sourcing good class ponies for clients both at home and abroad. A more recent project has been with the assistance of Mary McCann of Hartwell Stud to complete an artificial insemination project with her champion stallion Tulira Robuck, so that he can contribute to the breed particularly in America. The Tulira Connemara Pony Stud is known all over the pony world, and so is Lady Anne Hemphill, as she has made such a huge contribution to the breed, so much so that the there are very few countries that Connemara ponies do not have a Tulira prefix somewhere in their bloodlines.

Lady Molly Cusack-Smith and Lady Anne Hemphill

Iris Kellett

During her riding career Iris Kellett was one of the most stylish and successful showjumping riders in the world. A regular member of the Irish Showjumping Team, it was as an individual that she won the Princess Elizabeth Cup at the White City in London in 1948, and later she won the European Championship at the Royal Dublin Society Horse Show in Dublin in 1969.

She is a well known trainer of showjumping riders, and amongst those that she tutored that went on to International honours were Eddie Macken, Paul Darragh, Jack Doyle and Peter Charles to name but a few.

She is the recipient of many awards, an Honorary Doctorate degree from the University of Limerick for her work as an advisor on the preparation of their equestrian science degree, and the Irish Sports Council elected her to the Irish Sports Council Hall of Fame.

Much has been written about Iris Kellett and her achievements in showjumping, in breeding competition horses and training young riders. Meeting with her I was fascinated even more at how she started out her career in horses, and her description of life in those early days. For such a genteel lady I found it difficult to believe that she was so resilient, but as one of her fellow competitors remarked, she was always very determined to be the best, and she only settled for the best. She has been honoured many times over the years, with an Honorary Doctorate from Limerick University for her work in acting as an advisor on the equestrian science degree in the college.

She also took a keen interest in Riding for the Disabled, and in 1997 was elected to the Irish Sports Hall of Fame.

The Early Days in Mespil Road

Iris Kellett was an only child, which she says is just as well as she had three ponies, and she did not have to share them with any brothers and sisters. Her father Harry was a Veterinary Surgeon who served in the First World War, and he was so appalled at the suffering and inhumanity to animals, that he did not practice when he returned, but instead went into business. Her mother Dolly's family did not keep horses, but she was always very supportive even though she had been in bad health for some time, and unfortunately she passed away when Iris was very young. Her father had a passionate interest in horses. Life was busy living on their four acres equestrian complex in Mespil Road, Dublin close to Baggot Street Bridge, in the most expensive residential area in Dublin City. At an early age Iris was determined to be self sufficient, and as a teenager she started teaching children in the area to ride ponies, and then graduated to running early morning rides for businessmen on their way to work in the city. She built what was probably the first indoor arena in Ireland about the same time, mainly made of plywood, and costing £40 in total. It was round in shape, not very big, but was ideal for teaching in bad weather. The large indoor arena was built much later, and together with Burton Hall were the only indoor arenas at the time in Ireland. The operation grew so much in Mespil with the numbers of horses and students increasing all the time, that Gus O'Brien delivered a load of hay all the way from Summerhill in County Meath every day. Her father had a keen interest in point to pointers as had Iris, so they mapped out a gallop of two furlongs on the periphery of their property, so that when they wanted to canter the race horses for a mile it was four laps. She was never a reader but her father was, and although there were few books on teaching horsemanship at the time, he would recommend whatever was available on riding and teaching, and she would study all the different methods. In fact horsemanship and cooking were her two favourite pastimes. She got into horses very quickly and her ambition was to ride in point to points, but just when she had her first horse ready, the horse had a bad accident which she was very upset about, as it was to end her opportunity, which transpired to be to showjumping's benefit. Aside from the Royal Dublin Society Horse Show in August, Virginia Show was one of her favorites, where she jumped in the early years on horses like Dusty, Starlet and General Battle. However the ordeal of getting to and from the show was a different story. It meant a 5am start in the morning, hacking all their horses from their stables in Ballsbridge down through Dublin City to the railway station near O'Connell Street to load them on the cattle carriages. The horses were then fed through the port holes in the side of the carriages. Showjumping started in Virginia at 8.00am and would go on until 6.00pm. As it was usually too late to go back home, they would normally book into the local hotel and rise the following morning around 5 am and collect the horses for loading on the train, to be transported back to Dublin, and hack them from the station back to Mespil Road. Even to go hunting in North County Dublin and Meath it was the same ritual of hacking on through Dublin to get to the appropriate train station until horse trailers became more available.

International Competition Horses

Iris has no hesitation is saying that Rusty II was her star horse. Her father asked the then owner Nicholas O'Dwyer who was one of his clients if he would sell the horse to him, and reluctantly he agreed. The horse got a fall on the avenue at home and fractured his hip, but when he recovered Iris had a method of loosening him up before he went jumping. She originally noticed his true potential out hunting when she was watching him with some of her other horses jump a wall. Rusty gave it a couple of feet, so it was straight into showjumping for him. He was a big horse over 16.3 hands, a half bred and very narrow. Her recollections of Rusty was as a star showjumper, and a frequent winner. He rarely hit a fence and they went on to form a partnership winning her first International competition outside Ireland at the White City in 1948, by taking the Princess Elizabeth Cup later known as the Queen Elizabeth II Cup.

The first Civilian Irish Showjumping Team

It has to be remembered that Iris was one of those unfortunate people in terms of the era that she was at her prime as a talented showjumper. Irish Army officers represented Ireland in showjumping up to the 1950's, so she missed out as did many other civilians on representing their country until the first civilian team was formed. The lineup for the new civilian team was Iris, Jim Bryson, Noel Hayes and Joan Morrisson, and they represented Ireland at the Blackpool Show. In 1952 Iris had a near fatal accident exercising a horse, when she received a compound fracture of the leg which developed tetanus. But she cheated death and after a long layoff she worked her way back to health, and eventually to riding in competition again. The first European Championship for women was introduced in 1957 which was won by Pat Smythe on Flanagan. Both Iris and Pat Smythe had something in common, they both owned riding schools. Iris won The European Championship on her home ground in the RDS riding her chestnut gelding Morning Light in 1969. Again like Rusty he stood nearly 16.3 hands. The horse was later sold onto France to be ridden by dual Olympic Champion Pierre Jonqueres d'Oriola. It is difficult to believe now that women were not allowed to ride in the Olympics until 1956.

Iris produced many other good horses like Olympic Light and Sheer Delight that were out of her showjumping mare Red Sand. If she was buying a horse she liked to buy them broken or ready to break, in other words more than halter broken and well handled. The main qualities she looked for were movement and attitude when jumping on the lunge. A good front and shoulder, and limbs that would stand up to work. She liked to go to people she knew to buy her horses, as they were familiar with the type that suited her.

Reputation as a Teacher

Although she had taught extensively since she was a teenager in Mespil Road, she always had an eye for potential talent, as she was good at assessing the ability of riders. She taught in the classical style, with emphasis on a good seat and position, which one can observe watching any of her former students. Eventually she decided to move to Kill and set up a custom built equestrian center where she would have more space, as it became more and more difficult to take horses continuously to and from the centre of Dublin City. There were also problems on occasions when inconsiderate people would park their cars across the entrance to Mespil, causing difficulties accessing the centre, plus the fact that Irish Life Insurance were building a large office block beside her premises which caused increased activity.

Over the years many of the top riders were taught by Iris, names such as Eddie Macken who rode her well known horse Pele who had been Champion Hunter at Royal Ulster Show at Balmoral in 1971, and the Ladies Side Saddle Champion ridden by Fiona Kinnear at the RDS in 1972. Macken had considerable success on the International circuit on Pele, as well as narrowly missing out on the Men's World Championship at Hickstead in 1974, finishing as runner up to Hartwig Steenken of Germany. Other students were Paul Darragh who lived near her in Ballsbridge who also competed on Pele, and Jack Doyle who was coached by her from an early age. There are many more names of former students like Peter Charles, Mark Armstrong, Niall Talbot, Kevin Babington, Peter Leonard, Ann O'Grady and Damien Gardner, in fact the list just goes on. She also taught in the USA, UK and France, but there was always too much to be done at home to take up all the invitations she received. Her staff like head man Jim Smith and instructor Madelaine Byrne were very loyal to her, and stayed with her for many years. Madelaine runs her own thoroughbred operation now at Margurite Lodge. Many other staff stayed with Iris right through the move to Kill which grew probably too fast, and developed into a very large commercial operation. She later sold it on and moved to her present home in Rathmore which stands on over 100 acres.

Current interests

Iris Kellett still teaches, breeds and keeps horses on her farm in County Kildare. Currently she has some well bred brood mares, most notably a thoroughbred by Melyno, a French Guineas winner from the Aga Khan's Sharistani black line, who has produced a colt by Top of the World a full brother of Un Desperado, and son of Top Ville. Iris also has a Top of the World horse showjumping. On the half bred side she has a mare out of her good showjumping mare Skylight, that won the Millstreet Derby, produced a foal for the first time to Master Imp. She is full of praise for all the young talent around at the moment, and her conclusions from having attended Cavan and Kill Shows recently was that she felt the jumping was superb. One can only touch on some of her many achievements in life as a showjumper, a teacher, a breeder, a businesswoman and as a person that gave the people of Ireland much to be proud of.

On leaving I noticed an old travelling tack box belonging to Iris. The name plate just stated 'Kellett Dublin', and that alone demonstrates just how well known Iris Kellett was all over the showjumping world.

Iris Kellett winning the European Championship at the RDS, Dublin, Ireland

Aidan O'Connell

Aidan 'Suntan' O'Connell is one of the most flamboyant figures on the hunting scene today. Always impeccably turned out, with extraordinary attention to detail in fashion both on and off the hunting field, that he attributes to his family upbringing, and hunting with the County Limerick Foxhounds in the days when Lord Toby Daresbury was master. He can recall at one period hunting 40 days, and attending 40 black tie dinners afterwards.

Aidan has show jumped to Grand Prix level, trained racehorses and won numerous point to points as a jockey, and ridden three times in the famous Aintree Grand National.

A committed supporter of the qualities and temperament of the Irish Hunter. He is a much sought after Bloodstock Agent by clients that are planning to acquire an Irish horse for pleasure riding, or top level competition. He spends much of his time teaching cross country riding and pre hunting courses to groups around the world.

It's difficult to catch up with Aidan 'Suntan' O'Connell who is a larger than life figure in the horseworld. In recent years he is either travelling overseas teaching, foxhunting or crisscrossing Ireland sourcing horses to suit his many clients around the world.

O'Connell has led a charmed life, hunting, racing, teaching and as a bloodstock agent. He is a classic dresser, characterised by his bowler hats, frock coats with velvet collars, red hunting tails all individually hand tailored by Willam Frazer in Limerick. Indeed his dress sense has been a benefit to him on many occasions. One such occasion was as a student visiting Cheltenham Races he found that the entrance fee at the gate was £15, so he went down town and bought a bowler hat for £5 and wore it all week gaining entrance free not alone at the gate, but also to all the plush hospitality areas! He is an entertaining storyteller and raconteur, and has a great memory for people, places and occasions. Always a fanatical hunt follower, a man of the world, and a true free spirit, he would have stood out for his individualism in any era. It is difficult to believe that he was not on the short list for the lead role in the James Bond films, as he is considered by many to have as much presence as others who have occupied the space. And as for film plots, the producers could have centered a film around his real life experiences! He enjoys the fun of the chase, and his philosophy is to live for today. He loves the company of like minded people, and with his engaging personality, is extremely popular.

Life has been a roller coaster ride for him, as he has hunted with over 100 packs of hounds in Ireland, Britain, America, France, Germany, Holland, Belgium and South Africa. His race riding tally comes to over 150 races in Ireland, Britain, Germany and South Africa including riding on three occasions in probably the most difficult steeplechase in the world, the Aintree Grand National, and twice over the famous La Touche race over the banks at the Punchestown Racing Festival. His talents do not end there, as he has also ridden at Grand Prix level in showjumping.

But there is a more serious and business side to him. He is serious about the benefits of foxhunting to the development of the Irish Sport Horse, and to the contribution that it has made in developing the skills of so many talented riders in Ireland, competing on the world stage of equestrian competition.

Introduction to Horses

He was born in Cork as his father wanted his sons to play Gaelic hurling for Cork, but his family later moved to Limerick. His father was a main dealer for Austin Rover cars. Although Aidan wanted to study Veterinary Medicine, his father convinced him otherwise by providing him with a Jaguar car if he passed his Bachelor of Commerce exams. His premise was that if you could understand money you could employ a veterinary surgeon! He was popular in college particularly with the students who followed racing, as they enjoyed travelling in style in a Jaguar to the races.

He was given his first pony when he was 9 years old, and immediately started hunting with the Limerick Harriers, hacking to the meets, and often riding home through Limerick city after hunts in the dark.

His first good horse was a 3 year old that his father bought him called Suntan. He stood 158 cms, and was broken and backed. Aidan hunted him and took him showjumping. Now in his mid teens he won at Gort Show and such was Suntan's jumping ability, that he went from being a novice to nearly the top grade in one season. The following year 1967 he jumped in 44 shows and was in the money in 42 of them. At the Champions of the Year Show then held in Malahide he won £100 which was a small fortune to him at the time. Another win followed at Loughrea Show where he won the Grade B, and was 3rd to International rider Tommy Wade on Rolling Hills and Gerry Costello on Bluebell in the Championship. He went on to win in Ballinasloe, and added the Championship in Tipperary Show against all the top riders including the Army riders, and jumped 6 feet 6 inches at Cork Show.

As a child Aidan and his pals had autograph books, and he wanted to get the autograph of his Irish showjumping hero Seamus Hayes who won the first Hickstead Derby in 1961 and many puissance competitions on Goodbye by Renwood, and was leading rider in England in 1949, '50, '52. He remembered standing at the collecting pocket in the Royal Dublin Society for hours in 1963 for an autograph, but Hayes was mobbed with admirers and he could not get near him. "That's it", said Aidan, "I am going to ride at the RDS", and in 1968 he achieved his ambition and rode at the RDS and came third. The winner leant across and shook hands with him. It was none other than International rider Seamus Hayes his hero. The following year with his sights set on Hickstead he broke his leg in a freak accident at Kildysart Show. He had already won two competitions riding Corbally who was by Starburst. To win the last competition his horse had only to jump the last fence which was a big oxer facing into the evening sun. Unfortunately the horse stood off the fence and stumbled on landing, somersaulted, and broke Aidan's leg.

Point to Pointing
He maintains that the kick for him racing was galloping and jumping at speed, with race riding coming a close second to hunting. He rode Corbally by Candelabra in the Limerick Harriers Members Race, and won it, and also a wager of £30 at 5/1. He describes the horse as a star, the fastest horse he ever rode over banks. He followed that with winning the 4 mile Pierce Cup over banks and drains at Tomhaggard. Another bet on himself of £35 at 10/1 had him in the money again winning £350, which easily covered his university college fees. He went to lectures in a three piece striped suit and a bow tie, and was known as the fellow with the 'propeller'. He was also riding out three lots of horses four mornings a week on the way to college, and hunting three days a week. His dealing and betting was going well, and he bought a horse from Frank Costello and named him Lord Roseneath after his family home Roseneath. After jumping him at Cork Show an Italian bought him for a significant sum of money and sold him on to the Swiss champion and

Olympic rider Major Paul Weier. The horse later jumped Nations Cup, and was champion Swiss Eventer. With the money he bought three horses. One won a bumper race and he sold him on to Fred Winter. The second horse called Foreman was in the money 26 of 32 starts showjumping. Aidan rode him in all his competitions except the last one when International rider Paul Darragh jumped a double clear winning round on him. He was sold on to Switzerland. The third horse Loose Change won three chases. The initial gamble on Corbally started everything. He won the Pierce Cup again in Wexford the following year, but in 1971 his horse was asked to carry 15 stone, and was beaten into second place. Aidan felt that half bred racing was a great way of learning to ride properly. It was also an opportunity of racing against the great National Hunt riders of that era, like PP Hogan, Connie Vaughan and Billy McLearnon.

Still studying at Cork University and driving around in his Jaguar car with his racing pals, he went to look at a horse at 4 o'clock one morning after the Limerick Show Dance in Billy Flaven's with only the light from a box of matches. He bought him the next day for 650 guineas, and sold him the following October for 8,000 guineas, which was an enormous sum of money for a student at the time.

South Africa

For a change of scenery he set out for Australia, but got mesmerised by South Africa on the way, and decided to stay and do a post graduate course in Accountancy. Dining in the Inanda Polo Club he met some members of the Rand Hunt. They told him that it was the fastest hunt in the world. "That's news to me", said O'Connell asking if they had ever heard of the County Limericks. They would not believe that he already had race winners like Outstanding, Exceptional and Superb Suntan trained by Adrian Maxwell and ridden by Mouse Morris. They knew nothing about Irish trainers or jockeys. So he challenged the South Africans to pick the horses, and he would race them over any piece of country that they choose. After showing them a taste of Irish horsemanship owners were quick to give him their horses to school, and in return he was lavishly entertained at all the big social events. He was offered a horse that was a very difficult ride, and he eventually got the better of him by hunting him. He rode him in the South African Champion Chase in 1974, but he got brushed out through the wings three fences out by the eventual winner, before getting to the finish.

Hunting

His first love has always been hunting, recalling the sheer thrill of hearing former huntsmen of the County Limerick Foxhounds Lord Daresbury, or

Hugh Robards blowing hounds away, and just sitting in behind on a good horse that he describes as pure pleasure, 'a cocktail party on horseback'. As an example of the effort he will make to follow hounds, in one week he hunted six consecutive days in Ireland with the North Galway, the Duhallow, Scarteen, County Limerick, County Clare and the Stonehall with the Saturday being the most hectic. Stepping off his horse at 3pm, he jumped into a taxi in his full hunting attire to travel to Shannon Airport and catch a flight to Tampa, via Miami. The only item of clothing he removed was his champagne hunting tails, replacing them with his red ones as he asked the taxi driver to collect him the following Monday morning. Still with time to do some business, he sold a horse to a customer on the flight, and on arrival in Tampa got on another horse and hunted with the South Creek Hounds all day and attended their hunt ball that night. In the early hours of the morning he caught another flight back to Shannon Airport and was sitting on a horse at 11 o'clock on Monday morning at the meet of the County Limerick Foxhounds.

He brought the first group of friends to hunt with the County Limericks in 1975, hunting nine consecutive days out of ten. One of the party Charles Barrelet later became a joint master of the pack. During the period 1969 to 1989 he describes himself also as a professional gambler, and estimates that he won for 17 out of the 20 years. One large bet in 1973 and again in 1983 got him out on top. He had no respect for money, and saw it only as a means to enjoy himself. In one year alone, he hunted 96 days with 36 packs on 46 different horses in 7 countries. As a regular follower of a number of Irish packs like the Co Clares, the Stonehall Harriers, County Limerick Foxhounds, the Old Mill, Scarteen and the Kilkennys, he keeps a number of seasoned hunters around the country convenient to these packs. He now rides mainly for enjoyment and to teach, so he does not do as much schooling of young horses as heretofore.

Hunting in England one Winter, he hunted 6 days in succession. He was staying in the up market Savoy Hotel on the Strand. Arriving back one evening he rang for valet service. The valet arrived addressing O'Connell as Sir. He pointed to his red hunting tails in the wardrobe that needing cleaning. The valet looked at the red coat tails with the Limerick green collar and remarked, "Does Sir play in a band"!

When he is having fun he does not worry about time, as on another occasion when he went to England to hunt at the end of the season in March, and he was enjoying it so much that he came home the following October!

Another story of hunting again in England, when a member of a pack in the north of England saw him in his red hunting tails and top hat, he approached O'Connell commenting that it must be expensive for an Irishman to come and hunt in England. No he replied, explaining that he came over most weeks and stayed at the Savoy Hotel in London. Taking an instant dislike to the person who O'Connell described as 'Having a ready made look about him', the stranger continued to press him in disbelief. He pointed out to O'Connell as far as he knew, going into a long description of the art deco designed landmark Savoy Hotel on the Strand, founded in 1889, that boasts their first chef as the famous Auguste Escoffier, whose recipes most French cuisine is based on, was one of the most expensive hotels in London, as if to say how could O'Connell afford it. O'Connell replied that as an Irishman it was worth it, as he enjoyed having an Englishman serve him breakfast in bed!

He hunts a lot in America too, particularly with the Genesee Valley Hunt outside New York, and the highlight of last season was a 25 mile run on a coyote.

The Aintree Grand National

He took out a professional trainers licence for the flat and jumps, and bred and trained a few winners such as War Bonnet that ran in the Aintree Grand National in 1978, ridden for a syndicate by Dessie Hughes. At Ascot Sales he bought a cheap horse called Vindicate for a syndicate that he felt would get him around the Aintree Grand National in 1979, and backed himself £500 at 6/1. The horse somersaulted at the first, but he enjoyed the publicity in the Press about a fellow with a bow tie and carnation riding in the National. Syndicate member Pierre Doyle asked him to make the running so that the horse could be seen in the lead at the first fence as he had already sold a half share in him to a buyer in the bar. Aidan jumped out at the start at the front. The horse hit the first fence and Aidan was taken away in an ambulance with his shoulder kicked out. The surgeon took out an inch of bone and stitched him up. In a television interview afterwards the interviewer said to Doyle that he must be terribly disappointed. Doyle's reply was "Actually no, sure our horse was winning the race when he fell"!

Deciding to have a crack at the Aintree Grand National in 1980 he got another horse, Our Greenwood from trainer Jim Dreaper. He hunted him all season and seven weeks before the Grand National the horse stumbled in a gap and broke his jaw and three teeth. Having recovered he went to the National having run in only one point to point, with Aidan wasting from 13 stone 2 pounds down to 10 stone 8 pounds. Aidan was very one handed as a result of the shoulder operation, and got his fitness back training with Limerick Football Club. To keep his weight down he ate nothing from Sunday night to the following Saturday before the race, except tea and champagne. Even though the ground was bottomless he was very confident after working out with fancied horses at Fulke Walwyns, and decided to have a joint bet with a friend of £2,200 to win £30,000. He jumped off smartly and survived the first circuit onto the final circuit. He was lying in the first four approaching Beechers Brook the second time heading for home. Another horse hit him and bumped him jumping Valentines Brook and he lost his stirrups. Having to jump the next without stirrups, he was pushed to last of the 23 runners. He confesses he panicked now as he recovered to fifth place, and instead of thinking of winning his £15,000 he pushed on at the next fence, which was the smallest on the course instead of steadying and balancing the horse. Unfortunately both of them fell over, and only for the fall he felt that he should have finished probably about third in the race.

He sold Our Greenwood as he was now 13 years old, and because of the strain of making the National weights. Hunting with the Belvoir Foxhounds in England one day Prince Charles the Prince of Wales suggested to him that perhaps as preparation that Aidan should ride in the Grand Military Cup a race specifically for British Armed Forces. Aidan replied tongue in cheek to Prince Charles, that "The army that I would be representing, may not be that popular with your mother"! As he wanted to be in with a better chance in Aintree he got a horse called Chumson from Fred Winter that won over fences in New Zealand. The horse was described as having one gear, and as a dangerous horse to race. He had great scope, but was unpredictable. The owners thought that maybe a competent hunting man might get around the National course on him. On the day of the Grand National the horse hurdled the first and second, and hit the third fence hard but he still stayed on his feet. O'Connell thought that this was great as he may have learned a lesson, but his luck ran out when he turned over at the fourth. He ran afterwards in the Whitbred and when coming to challenge at the Pond Fence, he failed to take off, and ran straight through the fence. Still keen to get around the Grand National course he identified another horse for another crack at it the following year that was with trainer John Edwards, but he was withdrawn five days before the race.

When he stopped race riding he schooled horses from 1986 for Tom Roche Garland. Both Aidan and stable jockey Stephen Cox took them hunting and had great fun advancing their education.

Teaching

About 20 years ago he was asked by a German hotelier to teach him to ride across country, and to find a heavyweight horse for him. After some lessons he got him to hunt, and he was so delighted that he built a cross country course at his hotel. The hotelier began by organising residential groups for courses that ran from three days to a week. Aidan arranged for a video to be made of him jumping the Limerick banks and uprights, and the demand just grew from there. He is now booked up to a year in advance to run clinics, and the numbers can run as high as 48 participants on each one.

The main emphasis is on safety, on the premise that while you can't eliminate the risk, by understanding what is going on you can reduce or control that risk. He stresses it's a partnership and is successful when the rider understands how the horse does his job and lets him do it instead of interfering with him. Other aspects are the theory of safety on a horse, peer assessment, jumping upright and drop fences, accuracy, curve lines and rhythm. He then coaches students on how to jump a steeple chase fence at a gallop as the discipline is different to showjumping. Now he spends a considerable amount of his time running courses in different parts of the world.

He also likes to stress the importance of fitness to ride, and he himself runs about 25 miles a week as he maintains that leisure riding does not keep you fit, like schooling on gallops where the stirrup leathers are shorter and as he says "You would have muscles in your eyebrows doing it every day"!

Bloodstock Agent

On his travels to America in particular he is fascinated with how they are so impressed with the Irish Draught horse and its superb temperament. They consider that they are the horse of the future as it is all new to them, while some people in Ireland think they are a thing of the past. He believes the standard of Irish Sport horses is slipping, even though it is a very special horse, and top of the eventing tables since records began. He maintains that the Irish Sport horse was designed by the English, and produced in Ireland to carry a soldier in wartime, or a gentleman from 11.00 a.m. to 5.00 p.m. while hunting. He believes that we are better off keeping the term Irish Hunter as Continentals don't understand the term half bred, or three quarter breds. He can understand experimenting with warmblood horses, but the difference he suggests is that if you present an Irish horse with a problem he looks at it and tries to figure out how he can deal with it, whereas a warmblood reacts by thinking how do I avoid it. In terms of stamina when an Irish horses seems to be tired, with a bit of encouragement he will come back to the rider again. A lot of horses are he feels being bred without considering the market. He maintains that foreign buyers need to see how Irish horses deal with the serious challenges facing them hunting in the Scarteen and Limerick hunting country to really appreciate them. The qualities of Irish horses as he sees it are temperament, durability, stamina and good galloping. In a speech to a German audience, one of them commented that an Irish horse has no real movement. Well replied O'Connell, "They had enough movement when the British chased you around Europe for 300 years"!

He has sourced horses and ponies for clients at all levels, from hunters to show horses and racehorses. Many of the horses that he has sourced over the years have gone on to be top Olympic, National and International eventers and showjumpers. They include the Aintree Grand National winner Amberleigh House, show hunters Deep Impact and Amberleigh Ebony, eventers Esker Riada, Mister Mullins and Gormley now ridden by Belgian Karen Donckers. A more recent sale that he brokered was Paddy and Linda Downes gelding Dromelihy Imp, the Champion Three Year Old at the Royal Dublin Society Annual Show in 2006 to Tim Trembath and his daughter Charlotte for a future in the showring in England.

Members Racing

He wants to revive the traditional members foxhunter races, that were so popular before the professional element entered into point to pointing. He points out that people's physique are different today than 30 years ago. He recalls when he went to a social function during Horse Show Week as a 19 year old. At the time he stood just over six feet tall, much taller than his own age group. Now he says that he is looking up at young people, as the current generation are in general much taller and heavier. Therefore he concludes that most hunt followers who would like to ride over fences are too heavy to ride a thoroughbred horse. Consequently they will never get the opportunity to enjoy the thrill of riding over racing fences and natural courses, unless they get a new organisation in place. He wants to revive an old sport, that of foxhunter racing using the Irish Hunter, and he would eventually like to see it affiliated to the Equestrian Federation of Ireland, as another contributor to the promotion the Irish Sport Horse.

Questioned by a friend as to whether he believes in reincarnation, he replied that if he got four more chances to live his life again he would not do it as well as he has done it this time! Every day is the best day of his life. He maintains life is all about the chase, whether it is human, equine or business, and indeed he is a true exponent of his philosophy.

Stanislaus Lynch

Stanislaus Lynch was a huntsman, a writer, a poet, a sports journalist, a broadcaster, a lecturer and a breeder of Connemara ponies.

He has written six books, and is the only Irishman to win a literary award at the Olympic Games in Helsinki, and a Diploma for Epic Literature at the fourteenth Olympiad in London for his book *Echoes Of The Irish Hunting Horn*. His other awards as a writer are numerous. He broadcasted on national radio and was a contributor to sporting publications all over the world.

He worked for a number of years with the Irish Tourist Board as an Inspector of Equestrian Establishments, and was one of the first people to consign large exports of Connemara ponies to breeders in North America.

To lovers of the Irish countryside and its customs Stanislaus Lynch is the ultimate author and poet. Few writers can touch the emotions of the hunt follower in the way he weaves his pen to describe in such colourful and descriptive language, the richness of the countryside, the thrill of the chase, hounds in kennels, puppy shows, Autumn hunting, opening meets and point to pointing. His other writings are equally compulsive reading, especially his race meeting previews like Aintree, Punchestown and Fairyhouse. His insight of Irish Sport Horses and Connemara ponies, describing breeding lines and conformation, as well as the atmosphere of Irish horse fairs, including the incidents, and the characters, give the reader the impression that they can feel the reality of being there. He has a tremendous feel for the countryside, the various types of landscapes, hills, bogs and skies. Whether

Lynch was writing in prose, features or poetry, the sheer brilliance of his descriptive passages captivates the reader. The only regret is that he had not published more books, but then his books are now collectors items due to the fact that they are now in short supply. They have been published in eight languages in eighteen countries as far away as India, South Africa, Argentina and North America. After he passed away in 1983, he left one unpublished manuscript, which his wife Margaret will possibly publish in the near future.

Lynch was a genius with his pen. Who else could craft the words in his poem *Seen From My Saddle*

"If I could dip my pen in silver dew
And use that stretch of country as my page,
And fashion all my alphabet from shapes
Of winding streams, green banks, and long grey walls:
Then I would weave these symbols into words,
With woods and lakes as pauses in my script,
And use as blotting pad God's scented air,
When finished, if the fairies praised my task,
My joy would be complete.
                              For only thus
Might folk like me make effort to describe
The countryside I see...and ride...and love."

Or the following passage from his poem, *Hoof-Prints on Parchment*:

"For hoof-prints on pasture succumb to our rigorous clime,
But Hoof-Prints On Parchment would brighten the pages of time"

Background

Lynch was born in Ballyjamesduff in County Cavan, where his parents ran a retail business. Being from a comfortable family he attended secondary school in the fashionable Castleknock College in Dublin. From an early age his interests were hunting, horses, hounds and writing. Much of his early experience was gained from hunting his own foot and mounted packs in the hills of County Cavan, where there is a lake for every day of the year. It is easy to understand how much he appreciated the beautiful Cavan countryside when he wrote in his poem *The Hillmen* :

"Our home is in the up-lands
Where the Great Creator spills
His richest browns and purples
On our everlasting hills".

His early life in Cavan was occupied with producing show horses, and showjumping where he was quite successful in competition. He moved to Booterstown in Dublin in the 1940's, where he continued his writing. When the Irish Tourist Board (Bord Failte) were awarding grants to Riding Schools, Lynch was appointed a Board Inspector, and his work involved travelling around the country inspecting the various establishments. He also designed and wrote the copy for the promotional literature that was used to attract visitors to Ireland for hunting and riding holidays. Despite all his commitments he found time to manage a riding school in his old Alma Mater, Castleknock College which was at the time the only school in Ireland to have such a facility. He also managed another riding school at Butlins Holiday Camp in Mosney. He gave up writing in the early 1960's to concentrate on farming and breeding Connemara ponies, Irish Draughts and half breds at his farms in Clonee and Naas, but he also bred and produced young stock when living at River Lodge in Balbriggan and The Glebe in Balrothery.

Equestrian Journalist

Having hunted with over 100 packs of hounds in Ireland, Britain, France and the United States, and hunted and bred his own pack in County Cavan he was well qualified to write about the chase. His first stories were compiled as a child when the hunt followers arrived back to his parent's pub after a meet. He would hide under the table with a notepad and make notes of the conversations which became more exaggerated as the evening went on. Although many of his publications are on the topic of the chase, he was in constant demand by publications like *The Irish Field*, *The Leader*, *The Irish Tatler and Sketch*, *Social and Personal*, *Dublin Opinion*, *Horse and Hounds*, *The Field*, *Country Life*, *Field Sports*, *Riding Sports and Country*, *The Chronicle of the Horse*, *The Horse*, *Town and Country* and *Thoroughbred Record* to name but a few. He also wrote features on other equine related topics, show jumping, showing and racing. He reported from various Olympic Games and World Championships particularly on showjumping. Some of his articles have interesting titles such as First Hounds of the Season, Holding the Line, Hounds have Flown, Ireland a Huntsman's Paradise, Incomparable Aintree, Thrill of a Lifetime, High Jump Competition in the Royal Dublin Society, Getting Ready for the Dublin Horse Show and The Show of 1000 Horses.

As a man recognised as steeped in country traditions and land use, with the approval of the Irish Department of Agriculture he attended at the invitation of the French Department of Agriculture a U.N.E.S.C.O meeting in Paris in 1966 on the topic of 'The Use of Rural Space'. Afterwards he wrote a paper 'The Part of the Irish Farmer in Equestrian Tourism', on which he addressed a convention of a delegation of 800 members from 42 Nations. 'The Economic Value of Hunting to Ireland' was another publication of his that followed.

One of his interesting hunting articles written for *The Irish Field* was when out for a day's hunting with the Ward Union Staghounds he came across a souvenir of one of the most celebrated yet tragic figures of European history, Elizabeth Empress of Austria. She was a renowned beauty and fearless horsewoman, and travelled extensively. She spent two seasons in Ireland hunting with the Ward Union Staghounds and the Meath Foxhounds, riding occasionally a horse named Merry Andrew who won the high jump event at the Royal Dublin Society. A handkerchief that she dropped while hunting one day with the Wards, was at that time in the possession of Mr. Bobbit of Fleenstown House, Ashbourne, County Meath. Lynch's description of the handkerchief was interesting, stating that it was larger than a normal handkerchief, or a girls headsquare. But he summarised his description as, "It seems a perfectly serviceable piece of haberdashery, of cream colored silk, with a broad blue border flecked with small white floral designs, in the one corner her initial 'E' surmounted by her Royal Crown is embroidered in a design about two inches long." The Empress was married when she was 17 years of age to Emperor Francis Joseph. She disliked the Court and Official engagements, and was reputed to suffer physical pain when people tried to get a glimpse of her beauty. She stayed in Co Meath with Lord Langford of Summerhill and Lord Fingal of Kileen Castle. In the Spring of 1879 while hunting one day she is said to have jumped the boundary wall of Maynooth College, when the stag and the hounds entered a breach in the wall. When she returned to Austria she sent a silver statue of St. George the patron of England instead of Ireland's patron saint St. Patrick, to Maynooth College. Realising her mistake she sent a magnificent chasuble in gold of the Lamma Romana with the Austrian coat of arms embroidered on the back. Typical of Lynch's attachment to Cavan he was at pains to see if she had ever hunted in his native county, and managed to trace a reference through his father of a Mr. Eglintine Humphries, who kept a pack of staghounds at Lissagon House, Ballyhaise in Co Cavan. He was delighted when he found that the Empress had indeed stayed and hunted with Mr. Humphries during her visit, and performed an amazing feat of horsemanship when she jumped a lower outspread branch of a large tree on the lawn, with great accuracy. Sadly she was assassinated in Geneva on the 10th of November 1898.

Broadcaster and Commentator
He was a regular broadcaster on Irish Radio with commentaries from the Royal Dublin Society on the Aga Khan Showjumping Competition which

was the highlight of August Horse Show week, and the World Championship. But his broadcasting was not confined to equestrian events as he won the New Verse Competition for poetry judged by the well known Irish Poet Austin Clarke. Lynch's topic was of course horses, hounds and hunting. He broadcast his works also on BBC. His broadcast 'Background to the Irish Hunt' was described by presenter Eamonn Andrews as the best background documentary ever broadcast from Irish Radio.

He was a frequent lecturer to associations such as the Irish P.E.N. Club, the Blackrock Literary and Debating Society, St. Hubert Club in London, the Showjumping Association of Ireland and to Hunt Clubs in various parts of the world.

Publications and Awards

His published books are *Rhymes of an Irish Huntsman* published by Country Life and Scribers of New York in 1937, *Echoes of the Hunting Horn*, published by Talbot Press in 1947, *From Foal to Tally-Ho*, published by Dundalgen Press in 1948, *Hounds are Running*, published by Golden Eagle Books in 1950, *A Hunting-Man's Rambles* published by George Ronald in 1951, *Hunting Poems, Hoofprints on Parchment* was published by Wilson Hartnell in 1965, and reprinted by the Kerryman.

The book illustrations were by artists Tom Carr from Scotland and Michael Lyne from England. Interestingly Tom Carr was not involved in hunting, and such were the descriptive qualities of Lynch's writings that Carr was able to produce the illustrations from just reading the prose and poems without meeting with Stan or attending a hunt. Lyne on the other hand hunted, and held many exhibitions of his work which included paintings in oil and watercolors and bronzes of hunting and coursing scenes, including an exhibition Combridge's in Dublin in 1981.

Lynch also produced a book for the Irish Government in 1950 titled, *Hunting in Ireland*, and a record of Irish sporting activities for the Holy Year Exhibition in Rome, which were distributed around the world by the Irish Tourist Board.

Stanislaus Lynch is the only author in the world to be awarded two Olympic Diplomas for literature, at the London Games in 1948, and the Helsinki Games in 1952 for his books on hunting. He was awarded the St Hubert Gold Medal for his services to the literature of the chase by the Grand Chapter of the International Order of St. Hubert established in 1695.

Easons Bookstore in Dublin dedicated their front window to Lynch's Hunting Prints, which included models of horses and hounds and a display of his two Olympic Literary Awards. The New York Store Gimbels also held a week long exhibition of his works in their store windows. His poems have been included in publications such as *A Thousand Years of Irish Poetry*, *The Fox-Hunter Bed-Side Book and Concord of Harps* (Irish P.E.N. Anthology).

Although he had a home in the city of Dublin for part of his life, his love of the countryside is summed up again in his poem *The Hill-Men*:

"We've no envy for the city,
We were bred 'mong hills and rocks;
So we'd never barter freedom
For the servitude of clocks!"

Connemara Pony Breeder and Producer

It is interesting that Edith Sommerville who was co-author of *The Irish R.M.* exported Connemara Ponies to America in 1926, and found time to hunt with the Radnor Hounds in Pennsylvania while she was there. But Stanislaus Lynch consigned the first of the really largest shipments from Ireland when he sent out 54 Connemara Ponies in September 1959 to form the entire foundation breeding stock of Mr. Robert H. Wright's 430 acre Rose Hill Farm Stud, Georgia in America. He built it up to a herd of 200 pedigree Connemara breeding ponies, one of the largest studs of its kind in the world. As Lynch was sourcing the ponies all around Ireland, and as he was compiling the list and breeding details he found that one mare recommended to him had dubious records. He commented to the owner that he must have the most versatile mare in the world, as the records showed that she had three foals in the same year by three different stallions! The Connemara pony consignment to America was made up of light grey stallion Tarazan, Montully by Tully Lad, and the broodmare Pilgah Star the only strawberry roan in the consignment. The consignment also included the ponies Lasssie Doon, Bold Venture, Cregs Fantasia and Piper Star.

Such was Lynch's vast knowledge of Connemara ponies that Mr. Wright tried on a number of occasions to get him to manage his American Stud, but Lynch saw home as in Ireland. He was then invited to a tour of all the major Connemara Pony Studs in America and Canada.

Lynch liked the good Connemara sturdiness and was not happy with the introduction of Arab blood as he felt it made them too flighty, but he liked the Connemara cross with the thoroughbred that would produce a horse about 15.3 hands. He was in demand as a show judge in other countries such as England and America.

Lynch exported the mare Beauty Queen who won the Pony Championship of the Netherlands in Hertogenbosch. The mare was chosen to lead the parade in honor of Queen Julianna's Birthday Celebrations at the Royal Palace in Soest. The mare was by Lynch Law by Marconi both bred by Lynch, the latter was sold on to America and winning the Grand Championship of the USA, the Senior Championship and the Best Stallion over 3 years old and the Model Connemara. Gaeity Girl a foal out of Beauty Queen was sold to the President of the Connemara Pony Society of France.

In this passage from his poem *The Horse Fair*, which was then conducted on the streets of the towns in Ireland, he captured the atmosphere of the occasion,

> "Streets are filled to overflowing
> Horses coming, horses going.
> Footpaths lined by countless heads,
> Half breeds, mongrels, thorough-breds.
> Massive Clydesdales...plumply round.
> Aintree-looking sorts....unsound".

In 1959 Lynch was approached to find a pony for Walt Disney to feature in a film he was making called 'Darby O'Gill and the Little People'. Of course his immediate choice because of temperament was the Connemara pony. He found a nice 2 year old silver grey colt by Cill Ciarin out of Knockranny Beauty, a mare that he had sold on to a client in America the previous year. What he did not realise was that instead of shipping the colt out to America, he was to be presented to Mr. Disney at a banquet being hosted in the Round Room of the Mansion House which is the home of the Lord Mayor of Dublin. The young colt would be expected to climb onto a 60 foot long and 20 foot high ramp to a platform without sides for the presentation in front of hundreds of guests and artificial lighting. It was too late for Lynch to tell them that the wild colt had never been handled as he was reared on the mountains in Connemara, and the first time anybody handled him was when they were buying him. It took four men to hold him for an hour while he was being vetted, and he recalled that he was the only pony he knew that could hit the roof of a stable with his fore legs without hitting his head. Later he coaxed the colt to follow an old mare into the train carriage in Galway Railway Station, but arriving in Dublin it took seven men to get a halter on him, and get him into a horse trailer. It was remarkable that a week after roaming the Connemara Mountains, with some kind care and handling by Lynch that the little colt walked up the platform of the Round Room in the Mansion House to the glare of publicity and batteries of camera flash bulbs popping, as the celebrities surrounded the pony who became the star of the film premier. Afterwards he walked down the ramp to the rapturous applause of the assembled guests.

Another of his poems features a horse sale, where the master has died, and his hunt horses have to be sold titled, *By Order Of The Executors*.

" Lot one-twenty-three. Here's the last of this Stud.
Now ladies and gentlemen, what shall I say?
Fifty guineas to start? for this rare piece of blood-
Fifty? Thank you , sir. Sixty...a wonderfull grey
Has been thoroughly hunted, is warranted sound.
Thank you - seventy. Eighty. The bid's on my right.
This type of hunter is hard to be found."

An interesting footnote is that Stanislaus Lynch was travelling on, and photographed the train in Finland that covered its windows with steel shutters as it approached the then occupied Russian Fortress near Hango, an act that is reputed to have given rise to the term 'Iron Curtain'. In an effort to find out if any of their Olympic horses were related to Irish stallions previously sent to Russia in the Czarist days, he visited the Russian Stables in the Helsinki Olympics village, and despite the segregation of the Russian competitors, Lynch spent an evening with them, which at that time was considered unwise, but he enjoyed talking and being entertained by the team.

We are fortunate that Stanislaus Lynch left such a legacy of literature, the first of which was *Rhymes of an Irish Huntsman* with illustrations by Michael Lyne and the foreword by Lord Dunsany, and *The Incomparable Connemara*, were selected by the Irish Department of Education for inclusion in the optional list of books for Irish schools

His wife Margaret was a well known follower of the chase herself, hunting occasionally with the Meath Foxhounds, the Fingal Harriers and the Ward Union Staghounds. As all of her husband's published books are now collectors items, many will anxiously look forward to the launch date of his as yet unpublished book, *In Search Of The Kerry Beagle*, which is written in three sections, the Kerry Beagle as a Draghunting Hound, as a Foot Harrier, and as a Fox Hunting Hound, which is a very important publication for hound enthusiasts by this exceptional, gifted and talented Irish writer.

In his poem *Cavan Patchwork*, he describes the landscape of his native country as like a quilt, he writes,

"In years to come when I am dead
Should someone tear that quilt apart,
Sewn-in by mem'ry's golden thread,
There they will find...a huntsman's heart".

George Watson

George Watson was born into a landed gentry family in County Carlow, where his father and brother held the mastership of the County Carlow Foxhounds for 92 seasons.

He was bound for an army life, but instead decided to emigrate to Australia in 1850 during the period of the gold rush at Ballarat north of Melbourne with Sarah Jane Townsend who he married shortly after their arrival. On the ship that transported them he took out a number of foxhounds from his fathers kennels and founded the Melbourne Foxhounds.

He was one of a group of people that founded the Victoria Racing Club, that went on to develop Flemington Racecourse, and he was the official starter of the Melbourne Cup for 35 years. His other business interests included Kirk's Horse Bazaar specialising in livery and horse sales, and Cobb & Co a mail coach service that supplied the gold fields and the surrounding areas of Victoria in Australia.

In recent years there has been a strong racing association between Ireland and Australia because of the Melbourne Cup, a handicap race run every year over $1^1/_2$ miles on the famous Flemington Racecourse on the outskirts of the City of Melbourne. Trainer Dermot Weld, owner Michael Smurfit and jockey Michael Kinane were the first successfull combination from the Western Hemisphere with horses like Vintage Crop followed by Media Puzzle ridden by Damien Oliver to win the blue ribbon of Australian racing. Weld's other placed horse Vinnie Roe, owned by the film director Jim Sheridan came close, and was extremely popular with racegoers in both Ireland and Australia. Their track record has been acknowledged as a tremendous feat of riding and training.

The first race meeting in Melbourne was in 1838 with the track starting at the site of North Melbourne Railway Station, and finishing at the foot of Batman Hill, now Spencer Street Station. Betting was originally wagered in bottles of rum. The track was moved to the current site at Flemington in 1840, but it was not until 1861 that the first Melbourne Cup was run. In 1864 Flemington came under the control of the Victoria Racing Club and a horse called Lantern won the inaugural race.

But the connection with Ireland and the Melbourne Cup goes back over 150 years when George Watson who was born in 1827 at the family home Ballydarton House, Fenagh, Co. Carlow emigrated to Australia as a 24 year old in 1850. Watson although from a wealthy landed gentry family in County Carlow, probably only realised his many talents when he reached his adopted land. He was an adventurer, a master of hounds, a businessman and above all a fine horseman and trainer. His father John and brother Robert were masters of the County Carlow Foxhounds for 92 seasons, and also were masters of the Island Foxhounds. They lived on the family estate at Ballydarton House, which is a short distance from Carlow town. His brother John was master of the Meath Foxhounds, and is credited with drafting the first rules of polo.

The journey out

George Watson was destined for the army, but instead he decided to seek adventure on the other side of the world. His journey to Australia is quite remarkable considering that when they sailed out they were at the mercy of prevailing winds, and the journey time usually took about three months. From the records I ascertained that he took a number of foxhounds out with him, and also a house in sections with a galvanised roof, that when assembled provided accommodation of three bedrooms as well as a number of living rooms. The house is still standing in Burnett Street in the St. Kilda area of Melbourne, and was recently for sale in much of its original condition. On arrival, he got married to Sarah Jane Townsend Watson who travelled out on the journey on the Lord Stanley from Gravesend in England with him, in St. James' Cathedral, Melbourne, and they raised a large family of eleven children, many of whom followed their father into hunting and racing.

Arrival in Australia

It was just after the Famine in Ireland but the atmosphere in Melbourne at the time was at fever pitch, with the gold rush in full swing at the Victoria Goldfields of Ballarat and Bendigo. Such was the influx of people seeking their fortune, that the city was dotted with various sizes of tents, which was the only form of emergency accommodation to house the bulging population. Initally to gain, as was termed colonial experience, Watson spent some time on a station in the bush belonging to W. and J. Payne at Western Point, and then at another station at Mount Sturgeon owned by a Dr. Martin.

But George Watson did not go into goldmining, but instead in 1852 he leased Kirk's Horse Bazaar from William Yuille on the corner of Hardware Lane and Bourke Street in Melbourne, where he ran a thriving livery and horse sales business providing horses for the goldfields, as well as the racing and hunting fraternity. Horses were also sold to other countries, for example he sold over 600 horses alone to the Indian Army. Mr.Yuille was closely associated with racing and compiled the first volume of the Australian Studbook. Watson was quite innovative in business, and added a feature that was new in the Australian sales ring. He insisted that all horses would be jumped over poles as part of the sales presentation which attracted huge crowds, and a corresponding increase in business. Another innovation that he added to the sales yard was a betting ring, which was unusual as Watson had a reputation for never betting himself. He followed this business venture with another business in partnership with Cyrus Hewitt, when they bought the horse transport business of Cobb & Co, winning the Beechworth Mail contract which carried a Government subsidy of £10,000 per annum, supplying the goldfields and the region of Victoria also with a mail coach service, the company that was known as Watson & Hewitt. They had no competition at that time as there was no railway system. He introduced the concept of changing horse teams at staging posts, which together with the new type of American coaches that had leather springs, were more comfortable for passengers, and could cover longer distances in a shorter space of time. He was well known to drive his own coaches for a wager. One such time was when he drove from Wangaretta to Melbourne a distance of 150 miles between sunrise and sunset. He was extremely successful as a businessman and particularly as a property owner, owning 5,000 acres together with various staging post stations.

The Melbourne Hunt

He put the Melbourne Hunt which is still the premier pack of foxhounds in Australia on a professional footing, providing the foundation hounds that he shipped over from Ireland. He added his hounds from two packs, one lot of hounds that he took over from a Mr. Jeffreys who was a squatter on the Murray River, and also from the Werribee and Corio Hunts owned by Mr. Pyke and Mr. Ferrers who decided at the time to leave the Colony. He structured a breeding policy with the established bloodlines, and the stud book exists to the present day. As he had strong connections with many of the English hunting packs it was quite a regular occurance to have draft hounds from packs such as the Duke of Beaufort, the Quorn and the Pytchley sent to his pack in Australia. The hounds were kennelled at his horse sales business at Kirk's Bazzar in the centre of Melbourne, but they were moved later closer to his home in St. Kilda. He initially hunted kangaroo and deer before foxes were imported from Europe. They had a large hunting country especially around Brighton, Frankston, Dandenong and the Warribee Plains, and he was joined frequently by senior political figures including the Governor of New South Wales and other members of the business community, and the numbers of followers could range on any one day's hunting from 100 to 200 riders. Watson was a strict disciplinarian and insisted that hounds moved off from meets on time, giving rise to the saying 'Time, tide and the Melbourne Hunt waits for no man'. He was the sole master in his lifetime, hunting the hounds for much of that time himself, before handing over the horn in 1895 to his son Godfrey as deputy master. In the 1850's his two whippers in were Danny Callanan the top steeplechase rider at the time, and Martin Rice who was later hanged for murdering Watson's veterinary surgeon Anthony Green. A painting which survives today, was commissioned by Watson from the well known artist at the time Frederick Woodhouse of the master astride one of his favourite horses Blackboy, together with hounds and his whippers in. Woodhouse who founded the Victorian Academy of Arts, was one of the best animal and portrait painters of the time, and was very much in demand to paint racing scenes such as the Melbourne Cup before photography became popular. Although a renowned rider in his day, his hunting career was curtailed by some serious hunting falls. One such incident was a fall over a wire fence from his good horse Rocket, pinning him to the ground. He spent the night in his hunt livery as his doctor expected him to die. Making a remarkable recovery Watson was back hunting within six weeks with his arm in a sling. Another fall that was to finish his riding career was on a horse called Cavalier, again over a stiff wire fence. Watson from thereon followed by a horse drawn carriage. Today the Melbourne Hunt is still the premier fox hunt in Australia hunting the original Ballarat hunt country as well, under the joint mastership of Mr. John Masterton and Mr. Jeff Urie.

Racing

George Watson was naturally drawn to racing as he had a passion for the turf, and in fact he purchased his first horse a steeplchaser Wild Harry soon after arrival in Melbourne. It was as a result of a meeting of the Dog Club in the Mitre Tavern that the Victoria Amateur Turf Club was formed. The betting ring was first established in Kirk's Horse Bazaar under Watson, with Tom Coker and J.J. Miller calling the odds. It was felt that race meetings at Flemington and Caulfield were not complete without the presence of George Watson, or his racing colours of cerise and black cap.

As a horseman he was often described as, having matchless hands, a perfect seat, and the power to make the best of good horse or a bad one, with skill and determination. He rode all his horses in a bridoon for more control so he could turn a horse quickly. He had considerable success as a rider, trainer and as an owner. Amongst his list of successes' were the Phahran Steeplechase with The Doctor who won 14 chases in succession, the Victoria Derby and VRC Oaks double with Flying Colours in 1860, the Oaks with Palestine in 1861 just a few days after the first running of the Melbourne Cup. He won the Town Plate and the Queen's Plate on Shadow in 1854. Shadow was such a prolific winner on the flat that it sparked debates on the need for handicap races, and it is felt that this debate contributed to the foundation of the best known handicap in the southern hemisphere, the Melbourne Cup. Other winners were Emerald who won the Great Metropolitan Steeplechase in 1854, Faugh A Ballah, Irish Blackguard and Ballarat that he bought from the poet Adam Lindsay Gordon who was a follower of the Melbourne Hunt. Another of his horses Banker he rode to win numerous races on the racecourses of Victoria, Campbelltown and Tasmania. When he travelled to Tasmania to buy a horse named Lottery, the owner insisted that he would not sell him unless Watson rode him in perhaps the most prestigeous race over fences in the colony, the Campbelltown Steeplechase. Watson won the race and went on to win the Melbourne Hunt Cup in 1857 on the horse, which he won again later on two occasions on Jumbo in 1860 and the Banker in 1866. Watson's stable was at its strongest in the mid 1860's as he won six of the eight major steeplechases, and was placed in the two remaining.

Together with J.J.Haywood he saved the present Caulfield Racecourse from becoming a cemetery. By chance George Watson was riding along by the Saltwater River to a race meeting which was being held at Geelong the following day. As he passed by Caulfield, which was then known as the Heath, he observed engineers surveying the land, only to discover that the local authorities had non-racing plans for the site. He turned his horse around and rode back to Melbourne where he arranged with some friends to form a deputation to Sydney, as Melbourne was then in the colony of New South Wales. They managed to have the sale cancelled. At the same time Haywood quickly put a race card together and took it over to Watson at Kirk's Horse Bazzar, and although they had been running races at Ballarat and Geelong they really had no course of their own. The group formed the

Victoria Amateur Turf Club with Watson and others as trustees, and they got agreement from the authorities to take over the site, and racing won the day. They went on to run three race meetings there that year, establishing Caulfield as a popular race course which it is to the present day.

But it was as a founding member of the Victoria Racing Club in 1864, when he was appointed as honorary starter of the Melbourne Cup, and paid starter from 1867, an office he was to occupy for 35 years and for which he is best remembered. For this he earned the title 'Prince of Starters', and for his race riding success, the 'Duke of Jumping'. He passed on his starter skills to his sons, Tom who acted as starter in Sydney, and Godfrey as starter in Melbourne succeeding him in 1896. He could be very firm with jockeys, as in 1891 when Malvolio won the Melbourne Cup he fined all the jockeys £10 each for disobedience. When the first starting gates known as the Johnson Gleeson Starting Machine was introduced in 1893, he accepted it very positively and believed that it was progress, and much fairer to owners, trainers and jockeys.

The success of Flemington attracted spectators to travel to it by river steamer as it was possible to gain access to the racecourse in the early years by the Salt Water River. They were entertained by the Christy Minstrels, and arriving the worse for wear because illegal drink was often available, and it was not uncommon to hear 'Man overboard' during the crossing. Many others arrived on horseback and by horse drawn coaches of all varieties. There were bakers' carts, dog carts, butchers' carts, all rushing to the course so that they could take up a good viewing position. One of the largest coaches was the Leviathan, which was drawn by 22 horses plaited and decorated with coloured ribbons and rosettes, driven in pairs, and accommodating up to 89 passengers. It was a familiar sight on race day to see the coach drivers performing displays in front of the stands doing figures of eight to the applause of the large crowds. The coach drivers were celebrities in their own right for their skill in managing such a large team of horses, the most famous of which were, Robert Grover, 'Big' Sampson, Levi Rich and 'Cabbage Tree' Ned Devine. A number of them worked for George Watson's coaching company Cobb & Co.

Robert Bagot

Another Irishman Robert Bagot from Fonstown in County Kildare that Watson went to school with in Kilkenny College in Ireland, but who emigrated to Australia ahead of Watson was the first paid Secretary of the Victoria Racing Club in Melbourne. A civil engineer by profession, he came to notice for his work in 1861 on the Melbourne Cricket Ground that gave rise to its oval shape that lasts to this day. George Watson through the V.R.C.

hired Bagot to redevelop Flemington Racecourse on the Yarra River which was causing flooding on the track. After he improved the track, he introduced a number of initiatives that led to the success of the course, like new parking facilities, new stands and a lawn area with the seating from the old stands strategically placed around the lawns so families could have picnics. He followed this by giving complimentary entrance to ladies, on the basis that if he encouraged them to come racing their families would follow. Within twelve months he had doubled the attendance figures. Another breakthrough came in 1875, when he managed to have the Melbourne Cup run on the Prince of Wales' Birthday, which was a public holiday on the first Tuesday in November. It was an instant success, so much so that within three years there was no mention of the Prince of Wales' birthday, it was from then on known as Melbourne Cup Day. By 1857 improvements in facilities were made for the Committee, Stewards and the Press. Jockeys were not forgotten in the upgrade plans, as an infirmary for medical treatment was built, including residential facilities for jockeys recuperating from riding accidents, which because it was built on the high point of the course gave the jockeys a grand stand view on racing days. In 1880 Bagot supported legislation to introduce the totaliser which regularised race gambling. Melbourne Cup Day attendances within 10 years had increased from 5,000 to nearly 70,000 as a result of all the improvements to the course. By 1880 that number had increased to 100,000. For his services to racing he was elected to the Australian Racing Hall of Fame in 2004, and on New Year's Day each year the 12 furlong Bagot Handicap is run at Flemington Racecourse.

George Watson left a large family of nine sons and two daughters, many of whom continued the family racing and hunting tradition. He made an enormous contribution to his adopted land of Australia, as a businessman, a horseman, and as somebody that helped structure the sport of hunting and racing that has stood the test of time. Perhaps the following record in the publication *Bell's Life in Victoria* on the 30th May 1857 describes just how adventurous and daring Watson was. At the request of the actor and theatrical impresario George Coppin that Watson trained for, it describes a function under the patronage of Mr. George Watson and the Melbourne Hunt on the previous Thursday evening as follows, "*A well known Sporting Gentleman, in rivalry in the famous dining-room, 1,000 pounds wager made by the Marquis of Waterford, will jump his celebrated steeplechaser Peter over a five barred gate, supported by chairs and in front of a blazing fire*". Some time later on the stage of the Theatre Royal in Melbourne, George Watson jumped a five bar gate on his horse Blackboy (stable name Peter), emulating the Marquis of Waterford's feat. He obviously survived, as he died at the ripe old age of 80 years of age. They don't make them like that anymore. Considering their antics, it makes the wildest of nights out in our terms look to them like a stroll in the park!

The pendulum has turned full circle with regard to the Irish association with the Melbourne Cup in the space of 150 years. Considering that George Watson emigrated from County Carlow in 1851, and was cofounder of the Victoria Racing Club that set the structures in place that has made the Melbourne Cup the biggest sporting event in Australia. I am sure he was very pleased to see the Irish trainer Dermot Weld, with Vintage Crop ridden by Michael Kinane and Media Puzzle ridden by Damien Oliver winning the Cup on the First Tuesday in November.

Watson's great great granddaughter Jan Cruickshank and her sister Margaret Coleman together with the support of the Victoria Racing Club introduced the George Watson Steeplechase race in 1989. Then in 1990 it was changed to New Year's Day and sponsored by the Victoria Racing Club and the Melbourne Hunt Club, when two other races were held in the memory of Robert Bagot and Captain F.C. Standish who was one of the founders and chairman of the VRC, and was also Chief Commissioner of Police in Melbourne. Before emigrating to Australia Standish spent some time in Ireland on the staff of the then Lord Lieutenant of Ireland. The Watson race is now known as the George Watson Hurdle Race and held in Flemington in July. It is a fitting tribute to this extraordinary horseman and businessman, who many people feel that it is only a matter of time before he is inducted into the Australian Racing Hall of Fame.

George Watson
'Prince of Starters'
at Flemington
Racecourse,
Melbourne,
Australia

Bibliography

SOURCES

Newspapers and Magazines
The Irish Field, Siobhan English
The Sunday Age, Australia, David Moore 1996
The Globe, Australia, 9th October 1940
The Sun and Guardian, Australia, 22nd October 1933.

Libraries
The Royal Dublin Society Library, Gerard Whelan.
The State Library of Victoria, Melbourne, Australia.

Secondary Sources
Bagot, Robert., *A Man Ahead Of His Time*, Biographical Note, Tony Robinson M.P.

Baily's Hunting Directory 2003-2004, Pearson Publishing Ltd., 2003.

Baily's Hunting Directory 2004-2005, Pearson Publishing 2004.

Bell, Isaac., *A Huntsmans Log*, (Charles Scribner's Sons, New York, 1947)

Briscoe, George., *The Best of Times*, (Bellinter Bridge Publications, Ireland, 2005.)

Cairnduff Maureen.,*Who's Who in Ireland*, (Hibernian Publishers 1991).

Clayton, Michael., *The Complete Book on Showjumping*, (William Heinemann Ltd., 1975.)

Herbert, Ivor., O'Brien, Jacqueline., *Vincent O'Brien's Great Horses*. (Pelham Books.)

Holland, Anne., *Hunting*, (Little, Brown and Company 2003.)

Holland, Anne., *Steeplechasing, A Celebration of 250 Years*, (Little, Brown and Company 2001.)

Huston, John., *An Open Book*, (First Published USA, Alfred A, Knopf 1980) (Macmillan London 1881)

Lynch, Stanislaus., *Hounds are Running*, (Golden Eagle Books.)

Lynch, Stanislaus., *Hunting Poems, Hoof-Prints On Parchment*, (The Kerryman Ltd.)

Mahony, Edmund., *The Galway Blazers, Memoirs*, (Kenny Bookshops Ltd. 1979)

McCheane, Des., Smith, Cyril., *An Irish Hunting Scrapbook*, (Sedryc Publications, 2005.)

Mohr, Nancy. L., *The Lady Blows a Horn*, (Sevynmor Press 1995.)

Ryan, Thady., *My Privileged Life*, (The Derrydale Press.)

Snoddy, Theo., *Dictionary of Irish Artists*, 20th Century, (Merlin Publishing.)

Watson, S.J,. *Three Days Full*, (Bord na gCapall/ Irish Horse Board.)

Willis, Grania., *Total High*, (Red Rock Press ,Ireland, 2005.)

Images
Acknowledged on Illustration page.

Footnote
The publishers have made every effort to credit the copyright holders of all material reproduced in this book, and they regret any omission that have occurred. If there is anybody we failed to reach we invite them to contact us. All photographs remain the copyright of the original photographer, and other images the copyright of the originator.

County Limerick Foxhounds on the road at Killmallock.

Mary Kehoe Master and Huntsman of the Bree Foxhounds with followers on the hill at Boromount

Foot Beagle Followers at Stradbally Hound Show

Ivan Dowling Huntsman of Mr Stewart's Cheshire Hounds in Pennsylvania riding 'With Anticipation' winner of six Group 1 races and $3 million in prizemoney. Also L. to R. Niall Molloy, Paddy Nielson and Sam Clifton.

American visitors to the Duhallow Foxhounds Beth La Motte, Daphne Nielson, Stephen Gross and Peter Blanner.

Fingal Harriers Joint Masters Laurence Flynn and Brian Beggan with Whip Kevin McGuinness and Huntsman Chris Smith.

Heidi Oldenshaw, Lisa Lambert and Ann Walsh hunting with the Kilkenny Foxhounds.

John Lyons and his sons Alex and Josh at the Fingal Harriers Childrens Meet at Donabate.

Kathleen Crompton hunting with the Cheshire Hounds in Pennsylvania.

Sean Kilkenny Huntsman of the Kilkenny Foxhounds at Kimacow.

Stuart and Kathy Malone hunting with the Cheshire Hounds in Pennsylvania.

John Duffy and Michael Bailey Joint Masters of the Ward Union Staghounds with the followers at Bellewstown.